BRETT MCDOLLY

How To Ace an Interview

Transforming Interviews into Opportunities, Winning Strategies for Interview Success and Career Triumph

Copyright © 2024 by Brett McDolly

All rights reserved. No part of this publication may be reproduced, stored or transmitted in any form or by any means, electronic, mechanical, photocopying, recording, scanning, or otherwise without written permission from the publisher. It is illegal to copy this book, post it to a website, or distribute it by any other means without permission.

First edition

This book was professionally typeset on Reedsy. Find out more at reedsy.com

Contents

Introduction	1
The Psychology of Successful Interviews	8
Pre-Interview Preparation: Laying the Groundwork	16
The Art of First Impressions	25
Mastering Common Interview Questions	34
Advanced Interview Techniques	43
The Power of Questions: What to Ask Your Interviewer	53
Navigating Difficult Interview Scenarios	61
The Digital Interview: Mastering Video and Phone Interviews	69
Interview Follow-Up: Sealing the Deal	77
Industry-Specific Interview Guides	86
The Future of Interviews: Staying Ahead of the Curve	95
Interview Success Stories: Learning from the Best	104
The 30-Day Interview Preparation Plan	114
Conclusion: From Interview Success to Career Triumph	122

Introduction

In today's fast-paced, competitive job market, the ability to ace an interview has become more crucial than ever before. As you hold this book in your hands, you're taking the first step towards mastering an essential skill that can dramatically alter the trajectory of your career. Whether you're a fresh graduate looking to land your first job, a seasoned professional aiming for that next big promotion, or someone considering a career change, the power of interview mastery cannot be overstated.

Gone are the days when a stellar resume alone could secure you the job of your dreams. In our increasingly connected and complex world, employers are looking beyond paper qualifications. They seek individuals who can not only perform the job but also fit seamlessly into their organizational culture, adapt to rapid changes, and bring fresh perspectives to the table. This is where the interview comes in – it's your golden opportunity to showcase not just your skills and experience, but your personality, your potential, and your unique value proposition.

1.1 Why Interviews Matter More Than Ever

The landscape of recruitment and hiring has undergone a seismic shift in recent years. Several factors have converged to make interviews more critical than ever before in determining career success:

1. The Digital Revolution: With the advent of artificial intelligence and

machine learning, many routine jobs are being automated. As a result, employers are increasingly looking for candidates with strong interpersonal skills, creativity, and adaptability – qualities that are best assessed through interviews rather than resumes.

2. The Rise of Remote Work: The global pandemic accelerated the trend towards remote work, making effective communication and self-motivation crucial skills. Interviews have become the primary means of gauging a candidate's ability to thrive in a remote or hybrid work environment.

3. Emphasis on Cultural Fit: Companies are recognizing that technical skills alone don't guarantee success. There's a growing emphasis on finding candidates who align with the organization's values and culture. Interviews provide the perfect platform for assessing this cultural fit.

4. Increased Competition: With global talent pools and digital platforms making job applications easier than ever, competition for desirable positions has intensified. A standout interview performance can be the differentiator that sets you apart from equally qualified candidates.

5. The Gig Economy: As short-term contracts and freelance work become more prevalent, the ability to quickly establish rapport and demonstrate value in an interview setting has become invaluable.

6. Soft Skills Premium: Employers are placing a higher premium on soft skills such as communication, leadership, and emotional intelligence. These skills are difficult to quantify on a resume but can be effectively demonstrated during an interview.

7. Rapid Industry Changes: With industries evolving at an unprecedented pace, companies are looking for adaptable individuals who can learn quickly. Interviews allow candidates to showcase their ability to think on their feet and demonstrate their potential for growth.

INTRODUCTION

8. Diversity and Inclusion Initiatives: Many organizations are committed to building diverse teams. Interviews provide an opportunity for candidates to share unique perspectives and experiences that contribute to a diverse workplace.

9. The Experience Economy: Just as consumers seek experiences over products, job seekers now look for meaningful work experiences. Interviews have become a two-way street where candidates also assess whether the company can provide the growth and fulfillment they seek.

10. Personal Branding: In an age where personal branding is crucial, interviews offer a platform to reinforce and bring to life the personal brand you've cultivated online and through your resume.

Given these factors, it's clear that mastering the art of interviewing is no longer optional – it's a critical skill for career success in the 21st century. The interview is your stage to shine, to transform from a name on a resume to a memorable candidate who leaves a lasting impression.

1.2 How This Book Will Transform Your Interview Performance

Now that we've established the paramount importance of interview skills in today's job market, you might be wondering: "How exactly will this book help me?" Rest assured, you've made an excellent choice. This book is not just another collection of generic interview tips; it's a comprehensive guide designed to fundamentally transform your approach to interviews and significantly boost your chances of success.

Here's how this book will revolutionize your interview performance:

1. Mindset Shift: We'll start by changing how you perceive interviews. Instead of viewing them as nerve-wracking interrogations, you'll learn to see them as exciting opportunities to showcase your unique value. This

fundamental shift in mindset will boost your confidence and help you perform at your best.

2. Comprehensive Preparation Framework: This book provides a structured, step-by-step approach to interview preparation. From researching the company to crafting compelling answers to common questions, you'll have a clear roadmap to follow, ensuring no stone is left unturned in your preparation.

3. Psychology of Interviews: Understanding the psychology behind interviews – both from the interviewer's and interviewee's perspective – is crucial. We'll delve deep into the psychological aspects, helping you understand what interviewers are really looking for and how to manage your own psychology to project confidence and competence.

4. Storytelling Techniques: One of the most powerful ways to make yourself memorable is through effective storytelling. This book will teach you how to craft compelling narratives that highlight your skills and experiences, making your answers more engaging and impactful.

5. Industry-Specific Insights: Recognizing that different industries have different interview norms and expectations, we provide tailored advice for various sectors. Whether you're in tech, finance, healthcare, or creative fields, you'll find relevant, specific guidance.

6. Handling Tough Situations: Every job seeker dreads those difficult interview moments – whether it's explaining a gap in your resume or answering an unexpected question. This book equips you with strategies to navigate these challenging scenarios with grace and confidence.

7. Mastering Non-Verbal Communication: Did you know that a significant portion of communication is non-verbal? We'll show you how to harness the power of body language, facial expressions, and tone of voice to reinforce

INTRODUCTION

your messages and build rapport with interviewers.

8. Adapting to Different Interview Formats: From one-on-one interviews to panel discussions, from behavioral interviews to case studies, each format requires a different approach. This book will prepare you for all types of interview situations, including the increasingly common video and AI-driven interviews.

9. Post-Interview Strategies: Your performance after the interview can be just as important as the interview itself. Learn how to follow up effectively, negotiate job offers, and leave a lasting positive impression.

10. Continuous Improvement Plan: Interview mastery is not a one-time achievement but an ongoing process. This book provides you with tools and techniques for continuous improvement, ensuring that your interview skills stay sharp throughout your career.

11. Real-World Examples and Case Studies: Throughout the book, you'll find real-world examples and case studies of successful interviews across various industries. These practical illustrations will help you understand how to apply the principles in real-life situations.

12. Interactive Elements: This isn't just a book to be read passively. It includes interactive elements such as self-assessment quizzes, practice exercises, and reflection prompts that encourage active learning and help you internalize the concepts.

13. Expert Insights: Benefit from the collective wisdom of hiring managers, career coaches, and successful professionals who have sat on both sides of the interview table. Their insights provide a well-rounded perspective on what it takes to truly excel in interviews.

14. Confidence Building: As you progress through the book, you'll notice

your confidence growing. By the time you finish, you'll approach interviews not with trepidation, but with excitement and a sense of opportunity.

15. Long-Term Career Strategy: While the immediate goal is to help you ace your next interview, this book also focuses on long-term career development. The skills you learn here will serve you well beyond just landing a job – they'll help you in networking, professional presentations, and even in personal relationships.

16. Customization Techniques: No two interviews are exactly alike, just as no two candidates are the same. This book will teach you how to customize your approach for each specific interview, allowing you to present the most relevant and compelling version of yourself every time.

17. Ethical Considerations: In your quest to impress, it's crucial to maintain integrity. This book emphasizes the importance of honesty and authenticity in interviews, showing you how to present yourself in the best light while staying true to who you are.

By the time you finish this book, you will have transformed from an apprehensive interviewee into a confident, well-prepared candidate ready to seize every opportunity. You'll walk into interviews with a clear strategy, a positive mindset, and the ability to articulate your value proposition effectively.

Remember, in today's competitive job market, being good is not enough – you need to be outstanding. This book is your comprehensive guide to standing out, making a lasting impression, and ultimately landing the job of your dreams.

As we embark on this journey together, I encourage you to approach each chapter with an open mind and a willingness to step out of your comfort zone. The strategies and techniques you'll learn here have been proven effective

INTRODUCTION

across industries and experience levels. However, their true power will be unleashed when you put them into practice.

So, are you ready to master the art of interviewing? Are you prepared to transform your career prospects and open doors to exciting opportunities? Turn the page, and let's begin your journey to interview mastery. Your future self will thank you for taking this crucial step towards professional success.

The Psychology of Successful Interviews

Understanding the psychological dynamics at play during an interview is crucial for success. This chapter will delve into the mindset of both the interviewer and the interviewee, providing you with invaluable insights to navigate the interview process with confidence and finesse.

2.1 Understanding the Interviewer's Mindset

To truly excel in an interview, it's essential to put yourself in the interviewer's shoes. Understanding their perspective, motivations, and concerns can give you a significant advantage. Here's what you need to know about the interviewer's mindset:

1. Risk Mitigation: First and foremost, interviewers are looking to mitigate risk. Hiring the wrong person can be costly in terms of time, resources, and team morale. As such, interviewers are often focused on identifying potential red flags or inconsistencies in your responses.

Strategy: Be prepared to address any potential concerns proactively. If you have gaps in your resume or lack experience in a particular area, think about how you can frame these as opportunities for growth or highlight transferable skills.

2. Problem-Solving: Interviewers are often trying to solve a problem

within their organization. Whether it's filling a skills gap, bringing in fresh perspectives, or expanding the team's capacity, they're looking for someone who can address specific needs.

Strategy: Research the company thoroughly and try to identify potential challenges they might be facing. Frame your responses to demonstrate how your skills and experiences can help solve these problems.

3. Cultural Fit: Beyond skills and experience, interviewers are assessing whether you'll fit well within the existing team and company culture. They're looking for cues in your behavior, communication style, and values that align with their organization.

Strategy: Research the company's values and culture. During the interview, subtly demonstrate alignment with these values through your responses and questions.

4. Future Potential: Many interviewers are not just hiring for the current role, but also considering your potential for growth within the organization. They're looking for candidates who can evolve with the company.

Strategy: Highlight your adaptability, willingness to learn, and past instances where you've grown into new roles or taken on additional responsibilities.

5. Cognitive Load: Interviewers are processing a lot of information during the interview. They're listening to your responses, taking notes, thinking about follow-up questions, and trying to remember details about other candidates.

Strategy: Make their job easier by being clear, concise, and structured in your responses. Use storytelling techniques to make your answers more memorable.

6. Subconscious Biases: Despite best efforts, interviewers may have subconscious biases that influence their perceptions. These could be based on anything from your name to your appearance or background.

Strategy: While you can't control biases, you can focus on building rapport and finding common ground to help overcome potential prejudices.

7. Pressure from Above: Interviewers often face pressure from their superiors to find the right candidate quickly. They may be dealing with tight deadlines or specific mandates from management.

Strategy: Demonstrate your readiness to hit the ground running. Highlight instances where you've quickly adapted to new environments or made immediate impacts in previous roles.

Understanding these aspects of the interviewer's mindset allows you to tailor your responses and approach to address their underlying concerns and objectives, significantly improving your chances of success.

2.2 Mastering Your Own Psychology

While understanding the interviewer is crucial, managing your own psychology is equally important. Here's how you can master your own mindset for interview success:

1. Reframe Anxiety as Excitement: Interview nerves are common, but they can be debilitating if not managed properly. Research has shown that reframing anxiety as excitement can improve performance.

Technique: Before the interview, instead of telling yourself to calm down, try saying, "I'm excited about this opportunity." This simple shift can change your physiological response from threat to challenge.

2. Adopt a Growth Mindset: Believing that your abilities can be developed through dedication and hard work – a growth mindset – can significantly impact your interview performance.

Technique: View the interview as a learning opportunity rather than a test. If you make a mistake or receive challenging feedback, see it as a chance to grow rather than a personal failure.

3. Visualize Success: Athletes often use visualization techniques to improve performance, and the same can be applied to interviews.

Technique: Spend time visualizing yourself confidently answering questions, building rapport with the interviewer, and leaving a positive impression. This mental rehearsal can boost your actual performance.

4. Practice Self-Compassion: Being overly self-critical can undermine your confidence. Instead, practice self-compassion.

Technique: If you make a mistake during the interview, acknowledge it without judgment and move on. Treat yourself with the same kindness you would offer a friend in a similar situation.

5. Use Positive Self-Talk: The way you talk to yourself can significantly impact your confidence and performance.

Technique: Develop a set of positive affirmations related to your skills and interview readiness. Repeat these to yourself before and during the interview to boost your confidence.

6. Embrace the Impostor Syndrome: Many high-achievers experience impostor syndrome – feeling like a fraud despite evidence of their competence. Recognize that this is common and doesn't reflect reality.

Technique: Keep a "brag file" of your accomplishments, positive feedback, and successes. Review this before interviews to remind yourself of your true capabilities.

7. Focus on Connection, Not Perfection: Striving for perfection can increase anxiety and make you appear rigid. Instead, focus on building a genuine connection with the interviewer.

Technique: Approach the interview as a conversation rather than an interrogation. Show genuine interest in the interviewer and the company, and let your authentic self shine through.

8. Practice Mindfulness: Being present in the moment can help reduce anxiety and improve your ability to think clearly and respond effectively.

Technique: Before the interview, take a few minutes to practice deep breathing or a quick mindfulness meditation to center yourself.

By mastering these psychological techniques, you can create a positive mental state that allows you to showcase your best self during the interview.

2.3 Building Unshakeable Confidence

Confidence is key in interviews. It affects how you present yourself, how you respond to questions, and how the interviewer perceives you. Here's how to build unshakeable confidence for your interviews:

1. Prepare Thoroughly: Nothing builds confidence like being well-prepared.

Action Steps:
 - Research the company extensively
 - Practice common interview questions
 - Prepare specific examples and stories that demonstrate your skills

- Rehearse your responses out loud or with a friend

2. Know Your Value: Understanding and truly believing in your own worth is fundamental to projecting confidence.

Action Steps:
   - List your key strengths, skills, and unique experiences
   - Identify specific instances where you've added value in previous roles
   - Prepare to articulate your unique selling points clearly and concisely

3. Dress for Success: How you dress affects not only how others perceive you but also how you feel about yourself.

Action Steps:
   - Choose an outfit that's appropriate for the company culture but slightly more formal
   - Ensure your clothes fit well and are comfortable
   - Pay attention to grooming details

4. Power Posing: Research suggests that adopting confident body language can actually make you feel more confident.

Action Steps:
   - Before the interview, find a private space to stand in a "power pose" (arms raised in a V shape, or hands on hips) for two minutes
   - During the interview, sit up straight, lean slightly forward, and maintain open body language

5. Use Anchoring Techniques: Create a physical or mental anchor to quickly access a confident state of mind.

Action Steps:
   - Choose a physical gesture (like pressing your thumb and forefinger

together) or a mental image that represents confidence to you
   - Practice associating this anchor with feeling confident
   - Use the anchor before and during the interview to boost your confidence

6. Focus on Your Strengths: While it's important to be prepared for questions about weaknesses, dwelling on them can undermine your confidence.

Action Steps:
   - Spend more time rehearsing responses that highlight your strengths
   - For questions about weaknesses, have prepared responses that show self-awareness and a commitment to improvement

7. Celebrate Past Successes: Reminding yourself of past achievements can boost your confidence in your abilities.

Action Steps:
   - Before the interview, review your "brag file" or list of accomplishments
   - Mentally replay moments of past success to put yourself in a positive, confident mindset

8. Practice Positive Self-Talk: The way you talk to yourself has a profound impact on your confidence levels.

Action Steps:
   - Identify and challenge negative self-talk
   - Replace negative thoughts with positive, empowering statements
   - Create a pre-interview pep talk for yourself

9. Embrace Imperfection: Remember that interviewers are not expecting perfection. They're looking for competence, authenticity, and potential.

Action Steps:
   - If you make a mistake, acknowledge it briefly and move on

- Focus on showcasing your genuine enthusiasm and willingness to learn

10. Continuous Improvement: Building confidence is an ongoing process. Each interview is an opportunity to learn and improve.

Action Steps:
  - After each interview, reflect on what went well and areas for improvement
  - Seek feedback when possible
  - Continuously update your skills and knowledge in your field

By understanding the interviewer's mindset, mastering your own psychology, and building unshakeable confidence, you'll be well-equipped to excel in any interview situation. Remember, confidence is not about being perfect or knowing everything – it's about trusting in your abilities, being authentic, and showing a genuine enthusiasm for the opportunity at hand.

As you move forward in your interview preparation, keep these psychological insights in mind. They will not only help you perform better in interviews but will also contribute to your overall professional growth and success.

Pre-Interview Preparation: Laying the Groundwork

The key to a successful interview often lies in the preparation that takes place long before you step into the interview room. This chapter will guide you through the essential steps of pre-interview preparation, helping you lay a solid foundation for interview success.

3.1 Researching the Company: Going Beyond the Basics

While most candidates understand the importance of researching the company, few go beyond a cursory glance at the company's website. To truly stand out, you need to dive deeper and gain a comprehensive understanding of the organization.

1. Company History and Culture:
   - Study the company's founding story, mission, and values.
   - Look for recent news articles, press releases, and social media posts to understand current priorities and challenges.
   - Research the company culture through employee reviews on sites like Glassdoor or by reaching out to current or former employees on LinkedIn.

2. Financial Performance:
   - For public companies, review annual reports and earnings calls transcripts.

- For private companies, look for news about funding rounds or partnerships that indicate financial health.

3. Competitive Landscape:
   - Identify the company's main competitors and understand how they position themselves in the market.
   - Look for unique selling points that set the company apart from its competition.

4. Industry Trends:
   - Stay updated on industry news and trends that might affect the company.
   - Understand how technological advancements or regulatory changes might impact the business.

5. Key Leaders and Decision Makers:
   - Research the backgrounds of company executives and board members.
   - Look for interviews or articles featuring company leaders to understand their vision and priorities.

6. Products or Services:
   - Gain a deep understanding of the company's offerings.
   - If possible, try out the product or service yourself.

7. Corporate Social Responsibility:
   - Look into the company's sustainability efforts and community involvement.
   - Understand how these initiatives align with the company's overall mission.

8. Future Plans:
   - Research any announced expansions, new product launches, or strategic shifts.
   - Look for clues about the company's long-term vision and growth strategy.

9. Company Challenges:
   - Identify any recent setbacks or challenges the company has faced.
   - Look for how the company has responded to these challenges.

10. Company Achievements:
    - Note recent awards, recognitions, or milestones the company has achieved.
    - Understand the significance of these achievements in the industry context.

By going beyond surface-level research, you'll be able to engage in more meaningful conversations during the interview, demonstrating your genuine interest and understanding of the company.

3.2 Understanding the Role: Becoming the Ideal Candidate

To position yourself as the ideal candidate, you need to develop a deep understanding of the role you're applying for and align your skills and experiences accordingly.

1. Analyze the Job Description:
   - Break down the job description into key responsibilities and required skills.
   - Identify both explicit and implicit requirements.

2. Research Similar Roles:
   - Look at job postings for similar positions at other companies to gain a broader understanding of industry expectations.
   - Identify any skills or qualifications that consistently appear across these postings.

3. Understand the Department:
   - Research how the role fits into the larger department and company structure.

- Understand the typical career progression for this role within the company.

4. Identify Key Challenges:
   - Try to anticipate the main challenges associated with the role.
   - Prepare examples of how you've tackled similar challenges in the past.

5. Develop Role-Specific Knowledge:
   - Stay updated on industry-specific tools, technologies, or methodologies relevant to the role.
   - If possible, enhance your skills in areas crucial to the position.

6. Understand Performance Metrics:
   - Research how success is typically measured for this type of role.
   - Prepare examples of how you've excelled in similar performance areas.

7. Anticipate Future Trends:
   - Consider how the role might evolve in the coming years due to industry trends or technological advancements.
   - Demonstrate your adaptability and forward-thinking approach.

8. Network with Professionals:
   - Connect with individuals who hold similar positions to gain insider insights.
   - Use informational interviews to understand the day-to-day realities of the role.

9. Align Your Experiences:
   - Identify experiences from your background that directly relate to the role's requirements.
   - Prepare specific examples that demonstrate your ability to excel in key areas.

10. Address Potential Gaps:
   - Honestly assess any areas where you might fall short of the ideal qualifications.
   - Prepare to discuss how you plan to address these gaps or how your other strengths compensate for them.

By thoroughly understanding the role, you can present yourself as a candidate who not only meets the basic requirements but is also uniquely positioned to excel and add value to the organization.

3.3 Crafting Your Personal Brand

Your personal brand is the unique combination of skills, experiences, and personality that you want to convey to potential employers. Crafting a strong personal brand can help you stand out in a competitive job market and leave a lasting impression on interviewers.

1. Define Your Unique Value Proposition:
   - Identify your key strengths, skills, and experiences that set you apart.
   - Consider how these align with the needs of your target industry and roles.

2. Develop Your Personal Mission Statement:
   - Craft a concise statement that encapsulates your professional goals and values.
   - Ensure this aligns with the company's mission and the role you're applying for.

3. Identify Your Target Audience:
   - Understand the needs and preferences of your potential employers.
   - Tailor your brand messaging to resonate with this audience.

4. Craft Your Elevator Pitch:
   - Develop a 30-second summary of who you are professionally and what

you offer.
   - Practice delivering this pitch naturally and confidently.

5. Curate Your Online Presence:
   - Ensure your LinkedIn profile is up-to-date and reflects your personal brand.
   - Consider creating a personal website or portfolio to showcase your work.

6. Develop a Consistent Visual Identity:
   - Use a professional, consistent photo across all platforms.
   - Consider creating a personal logo or consistent color scheme for your materials.

7. Share Your Expertise:
   - Engage in industry discussions on platforms like LinkedIn or Twitter.
   - Consider writing articles or creating content related to your field.

8. Seek Speaking Opportunities:
   - Look for chances to present at industry events or webinars.
   - This can help establish you as a thought leader in your field.

9. Network Strategically:
   - Attend industry events and connect with professionals in your field.
   - Engage in meaningful conversations that reflect your personal brand.

10. Continuously Evolve Your Brand:
    - Regularly reassess and update your personal brand as your career progresses.
    - Stay open to feedback and be willing to refine your brand over time.

By crafting a strong personal brand, you create a consistent, compelling narrative about who you are professionally. This can help interviewers quickly understand your value and envision how you might fit into their organization.

3.4 Tailoring Your Resume and Cover Letter for Maximum Impact

Your resume and cover letter are often your first opportunity to make an impression on potential employers. Tailoring these documents for each application can significantly increase your chances of landing an interview.

1. Customize Your Resume for Each Application:
   - Align your skills and experiences with the specific job requirements.
   - Use keywords from the job description to pass through Applicant Tracking Systems (ATS).

2. Highlight Relevant Achievements:
   - Focus on accomplishments that directly relate to the target role.
   - Use quantifiable results to demonstrate your impact.

3. Organize Information Strategically:
   - Place the most relevant information near the top of your resume.
   - Use a format that best highlights your strengths (chronological, functional, or combination).

4. Craft a Compelling Professional Summary:
   - Write a brief, powerful statement that encapsulates your professional brand and key qualifications.
   - Tailor this summary to align with the specific role and company.

5. Use Action Verbs:
   - Start bullet points with strong action verbs to convey initiative and impact.
   - Vary your word choice to keep the reader engaged.

6. Include Relevant Skills and Certifications:
   - Highlight technical skills and certifications that are specifically mentioned

in the job description.
   - Consider creating a separate skills section for easy scanning.

7. Customize Your Cover Letter:
   - Address the letter to a specific person whenever possible.
   - Open with a strong hook that demonstrates your enthusiasm for the role and company.

8. Align Your Cover Letter with Company Values:
   - Reference the company's mission or recent achievements to show you've done your research.
   - Explain how your values align with those of the organization.

9. Tell a Compelling Story:
   - Use your cover letter to narrate how your experiences have led you to this specific opportunity.
   - Highlight 2-3 key experiences that directly relate to the role.

10. Proofread Meticulously:
    - Eliminate any typos or grammatical errors.
    - Consider having a trusted friend or mentor review your documents.

11. Keep Design Clean and Professional:
    - Use a clean, easy-to-read font and consistent formatting.
    - Ensure your resume and cover letter have a cohesive look.

12. Tailor Length Appropriately:
    - Keep your resume to 1-2 pages, depending on your experience level.
    - Limit your cover letter to one page, focusing on the most compelling points.

By tailoring your resume and cover letter, you demonstrate to employers that you've put thought and effort into your application. This attention to detail can set you apart from other candidates and increase your chances of moving forward in the hiring process.

Remember, pre-interview preparation is an investment in your future. By thoroughly researching the company, understanding the role, crafting your personal brand, and tailoring your application materials, you lay a solid foundation for interview success. This preparation not only helps you perform better during the interview but also demonstrates to potential employers your genuine interest, professionalism, and attention to detail – qualities that are highly valued in any role.

The Art of First Impressions

In the world of job interviews, first impressions are crucial. Research shows that interviewers often form their initial opinions about candidates within the first few seconds of meeting them. These early judgments can significantly influence the entire interview process and its outcome. This chapter will guide you through the essential elements of making a stellar first impression, focusing on your appearance, body language, and initial interaction.

4.1 Dressing for Success: Industry-Specific Guidelines

The way you dress for an interview sends a powerful message about your professionalism, attention to detail, and understanding of the company culture. While the specifics may vary by industry, some general principles apply across the board:

1. Research the Company Culture:
   - Look at the company's website and social media for clues about the dress code.
   - If possible, observe employees entering and leaving the office.

2. Err on the Side of Formality:
   - It's generally better to be slightly overdressed than underdressed.
   - When in doubt, opt for business professional attire.

3. Ensure Everything Fits Well:
   - Ill-fitting clothes can be distracting and make you appear unprofessional.
   - Consider having key pieces tailored for a perfect fit.

4. Pay Attention to Grooming:
   - Ensure your hair is neat and styled conservatively.
   - Keep makeup subtle and professional.
   - Ensure nails are clean and well-maintained.

5. Minimize Distractions:
   - Avoid overpowering fragrances.
   - Keep jewelry minimal and conservative.

Now, let's look at some industry-specific guidelines:

Finance and Law:
   - These industries tend to be the most conservative in dress code.
   - For men: Dark suit (navy or charcoal), white dress shirt, conservative tie, polished dress shoes.
   - For women: Suit (pantsuit or skirt suit), conservative blouse, closed-toe heels, minimal jewelry.

Tech and Startups:
   - Often more casual, but still professional.
   - For men: Slacks or khakis, button-down shirt (tie optional), dress shoes or clean, stylish sneakers.
   - For women: Slacks or a knee-length skirt, blouse or sweater, comfortable yet professional shoes.

Creative Industries (Advertising, Design, Media):
   - More flexibility for personal style, but still professional.
   - For men: Slacks or dark jeans, button-down shirt or polo, blazer, stylish shoes.

- For women: Stylish dress or slacks with a blouse, statement jewelry acceptable, fashionable yet comfortable shoes.

Healthcare:
   - Clean and conservative is key.
   - For men: Slacks, button-down shirt, tie, polished shoes.
   - For women: Slacks or knee-length skirt, blouse, closed-toe shoes, minimal jewelry.

Education:
   - Professional but approachable.
   - For men: Slacks, button-down shirt, tie, blazer (optional), comfortable dress shoes.
   - For women: Slacks or knee-length skirt, blouse or sweater, comfortable closed-toe shoes.

Remember, regardless of the industry, your clothes should be clean, wrinkle-free, and in good condition. It's also wise to prepare your outfit the night before to avoid last-minute stress or wardrobe malfunctions.

4.2 Body Language Secrets of Top Performers

Your body language can speak volumes before you even say a word. Here are some key aspects to focus on:

1. Posture:
   - Stand and sit up straight to project confidence.
   - Keep your shoulders back and chin up.
   - Avoid slouching or crossing your arms, which can make you appear closed off or defensive.

2. Eye Contact:
   - Maintain appropriate eye contact to show engagement and confidence.

- Aim for about 60-70% eye contact during conversations.
- When speaking to a panel, make eye contact with each interviewer.

3. Smile:
   - A genuine smile can help you appear approachable and confident.
   - Practice your smile in the mirror to ensure it looks natural.

4. Hand Gestures:
   - Use natural hand gestures to emphasize points.
   - Keep gestures within the area from your chest to your waist.
   - Avoid fidgeting or playing with objects.

5. Mirroring:
   - Subtly mirroring the interviewer's body language can build rapport.
   - Be careful not to overdo it, as it can appear insincere if too obvious.

6. Leaning:
   - Leaning slightly forward when listening shows engagement.
   - Avoid leaning back, which can make you appear disinterested.

7. Feet Position:
   - Keep your feet planted firmly on the ground.
   - Avoid crossing your legs or ankles, which can make you appear nervous.

8. Walking:
   - Walk with purpose and confidence.
   - Take measured steps, neither too fast nor too slow.

9. Waiting Room Behavior:
   - Sit up straight and appear alert, even in the waiting room.
   - Avoid using your phone excessively, as you never know who might be observing.

10. Facial Expressions:
   - Be aware of your facial expressions, ensuring they match the tone of the conversation.
   - Practice active listening expressions in the mirror.

11. Breathing:
   - Take deep, calming breaths to manage nervousness.
   - Breathing deeply can also help lower your voice, making you sound more confident.

12. Personal Space:
   - Respect the interviewer's personal space.
   - If shaking hands, step forward to do so rather than leaning across the desk.

Remember, confidence is key. Practice these body language techniques before the interview so they feel natural. The goal is to appear poised and self-assured, even if you're feeling nervous inside.

4.3 The Perfect Handshake and Introduction

The handshake and introduction often form the very first moment of direct interaction with your interviewer. Mastering this brief but crucial exchange can set a positive tone for the entire interview.

The Perfect Handshake:
   1. Timing:
      - Extend your hand as you approach the interviewer.
      - Make eye contact before initiating the handshake.

   2. Grip:
      - Aim for a firm grip, but not too tight.
      - Match the pressure applied by the interviewer.

3. Duration:
   - Hold the handshake for about 2-3 seconds.
   - Pump once or twice, then release.

4. Palm Position:
   - Keep your palm perpendicular to the ground.
   - Ensure full palm-to-palm contact.

5. Dryness:
   - If your palms tend to get sweaty when nervous, discreetly wipe them before the handshake.
   - Carry a handkerchief if needed.

6. Both Hands:
   - Generally, use only your right hand for the handshake.
   - In some cultures, using the left hand to lightly touch the other person's arm during the handshake is seen as warm and friendly, but this is less common in professional settings.

7. Standing:
   - Stand up if you're seated when the interviewer enters the room.
   - This shows respect and allows for a more natural handshake.

8. Practice:
   - Practice your handshake with friends or family to ensure it feels natural and confident.

The Perfect Introduction:

1. Smile:
   - Begin with a warm, genuine smile as you make eye contact.

2. Name:

- State your full name clearly.
   - If your name is difficult to pronounce, you might offer a phonetic pronunciation or a simplified version.

3. Greeting:
   - Use an appropriate greeting such as "It's a pleasure to meet you" or "Thank you for taking the time to meet with me today."

4. Interviewer's Name:
   - If you know the interviewer's name, use it in your greeting.
   - Be sure to pronounce it correctly – if you're unsure, it's okay to ask for clarification.

5. Small Talk:
   - Be prepared for a bit of small talk as you're led to the interview room.
   - Have a few neutral topics in mind, such as commenting positively on the office or expressing your interest in the company.

6. Body Language:
   - Maintain open, confident body language throughout the introduction.
   - Keep your shoulders back, chin up, and maintain appropriate eye contact.

7. Voice:
   - Speak clearly and at a moderate pace.
   - Aim for a lower pitch, which tends to convey confidence.

8. Listen:
   - Pay attention to how the interviewer introduces themselves.
   - Remember details like their name and title for use later in the interview.

9. Follow the Interviewer's Lead:
   - Be ready to sit when invited or to follow the interviewer to the interview room.

10. Be Prepared for Multiple Introductions:
   - In panel interviews, you may need to introduce yourself multiple times.
   - Keep your energy and enthusiasm consistent for each introduction.

Example Script:
"Hello, I'm [Your Full Name]. It's a pleasure to meet you, [Interviewer's Name]. Thank you for taking the time to speak with me today about the [Position Name] role."

Remember, the key to a great first impression is to appear confident, professional, and genuinely enthusiastic about the opportunity. Here are some final tips to tie everything together:

1. Arrive Early:
   - Aim to arrive 10-15 minutes before your scheduled interview time.
   - This allows you to compose yourself and observe the office environment.

2. Be Kind to Everyone:
   - Treat everyone you encounter with respect, from the receptionist to other employees you might meet.
   - Your behavior towards others may be reported back to the interviewer.

3. Have Materials Ready:
   - Bring extra copies of your resume, a notepad, and a pen.
   - Have them neatly organized in a professional folder or portfolio.

4. Turn Off Your Phone:
   - Silence or turn off your phone before entering the building.
   - Avoid checking your phone in the waiting room.

5. Stay Calm:
   - Take deep breaths to calm your nerves.
   - Remember that some nervous energy can actually enhance your perfor-

mance.

6. Be Authentic:
   - While it's important to be professional, don't forget to let your personality shine through.
   - Authenticity can help you connect with the interviewer on a personal level.

By mastering the art of first impressions – from your attire to your body language and introduction – you set the stage for a successful interview. Remember, practice makes perfect. Rehearse these elements until they feel natural, and you'll walk into your interview with confidence, ready to showcase your skills and qualifications.

Mastering Common Interview Questions

Preparing for common interview questions is a crucial step in your interview preparation. While you can't predict every question you'll be asked, there are certain questions that come up in almost every interview. By mastering these, you'll build confidence and be better prepared to handle unexpected questions as well.

5.1 Deconstructing the Most Frequently Asked Questions

Let's break down some of the most common interview questions and understand what the interviewer is really looking for:

1. "Tell me about yourself."
   What they're really asking: Can you articulate your professional journey concisely and relevantly?
   Tips:
   - Focus on your professional background and experiences relevant to the job.
   - Start with your current role and work backwards.
   - Highlight key achievements and skills that align with the job requirements.
   - Keep it concise, ideally 2-3 minutes long.

2. "Why do you want to work here?"
   What they're really asking: Have you done your research on our company, and can you connect your goals with ours?

Tips:
- Show that you've researched the company thoroughly.
- Align your career goals with the company's mission or values.
- Mention specific aspects of the company that appeal to you (culture, projects, innovation).

3. "What are your greatest strengths?"

What they're really asking: Do your strengths align with what we need for this role?

Tips:
- Choose strengths that are directly relevant to the job description.
- Provide specific examples of how you've used these strengths in professional settings.
- Be honest but confident – this is not the time for modesty.

4. "What is your greatest weakness?"

What they're really asking: Are you self-aware and actively working on self-improvement?

Tips:
- Choose a real weakness, but one that isn't central to the job requirements.
- Focus more on how you're actively working to improve this weakness.
- Avoid clichés like "I'm a perfectionist" or "I work too hard."

5. "Where do you see yourself in five years?"

What they're really asking: Are your career goals aligned with what we can offer?

Tips:
- Show ambition, but make sure it's realistic within the company's structure.
- Focus on skill development and growing within the organization.
- Avoid mentioning goals that aren't relevant to the company or role.

6. "Can you tell me about a time you faced a challenge at work and how you handled it?"

What they're really asking: How do you problem-solve and handle stress?
Tips:
- Use the STAR method (Situation, Task, Action, Result) to structure your response.
- Choose a relevant challenge that showcases your skills.
- Focus on your actions and the positive outcome.

7. "Why are you leaving your current job?"
What they're really asking: Are you going to be a reliable employee, or are there red flags?
Tips:
- Stay positive – avoid speaking negatively about your current employer.
- Focus on what you're moving towards, not what you're leaving behind.
- Emphasize growth opportunities and new challenges.

8. "What's your expected salary?"
What they're really asking: Are your expectations in line with our budget, and do you know your worth?
Tips:
- Research salary ranges for the role and your experience level.
- Provide a range rather than a specific number.
- Express openness to negotiation based on the total compensation package.

9. "Do you have any questions for us?"
What they're really asking: Are you truly interested in this role and have you been paying attention?
Tips:
- Always have questions prepared – it shows genuine interest.
- Ask about the company culture, team dynamics, or specific projects.
- Avoid questions about salary or benefits at this stage.

10. "What makes you unique?"
What they're really asking: What value can you bring that other candidates

might not?
 Tips:
 - Focus on a combination of skills, experiences, and personal qualities that are relevant to the role.
 - Provide specific examples of how your unique qualities have benefited previous employers.
 - Tie your uniqueness back to how it can benefit the company.

5.2 Crafting Compelling Stories to Showcase Your Skills

Storytelling is a powerful tool in interviews. It makes your answers more engaging, memorable, and convincing. Here's how to craft compelling stories that showcase your skills:

1. Identify Key Skills:
 - Review the job description and identify 5-7 key skills or qualities they're looking for.
 - Think of specific instances where you've demonstrated these skills.

2. Structure Your Stories:
 - Use the STAR method (explained in detail in the next section) to structure your stories.
 - Ensure each story has a clear beginning, middle, and end.

3. Keep It Relevant:
 - Choose stories that directly relate to the job you're applying for.
 - Focus on recent experiences, ideally within the last 2-3 years.

4. Be Specific:
 - Use concrete details and numbers where possible.
 - Instead of saying "I increased sales," say "I increased sales by 25% over six months."

5. Highlight Your Role:
   - While you may have worked in a team, focus on your specific contributions.
   - Use "I" statements to clearly articulate your actions and decisions.

6. Show Growth:
   - If possible, include stories that demonstrate how you've grown or learned from challenges.

7. Practice, But Don't Memorize:
   - Practice telling your stories out loud, but avoid memorizing them word-for-word.
   - Memorized answers can sound rehearsed and inauthentic.

8. Keep It Concise:
   - Aim to keep each story to about 2-3 minutes.
   - Practice trimming unnecessary details while keeping the core message intact.

9. Adapt to Different Questions:
   - Learn how to adapt your key stories to answer different types of questions.
   - One story might demonstrate leadership, problem-solving, and teamwork.

10. End with Impact:
    - Always conclude your story by highlighting the positive outcome or lesson learned.
    - If possible, relate this back to how it prepares you for the role you're interviewing for.

Example Story:
   Skill: Problem-solving

"In my previous role as a project manager, we were halfway through a major client project when our lead developer unexpectedly quit. This put us at risk of missing our deadline, which could have resulted in significant financial penalties and damage to our reputation.

I immediately called a team meeting to assess the situation. We redistributed tasks based on each team member's strengths and availability. I personally took on some of the coding tasks, working late nights to get up to speed.

I also negotiated a one-week extension with the client by demonstrating our revised project plan and committing to daily progress updates. This transparency actually improved our relationship with the client.

As a result, we delivered the project just two days past the original deadline, with no financial penalties. The client was so impressed with our handling of the situation that they awarded us two additional projects the following quarter.

This experience taught me the importance of quick decision-making, clear communication, and team collaboration in crisis situations – skills I believe would be valuable in the fast-paced environment of your company."

5.3 The STAR Method: Bringing Your Achievements to Life

The STAR method is a structured way to respond to behavioral interview questions – those questions that ask you to provide a real-life example of how you handled a specific type of situation. STAR stands for Situation, Task, Action, and Result.

Here's how to use the STAR method effectively:

Situation:
   - Set the scene and provide context for your story.

- Be specific about when and where the situation occurred.
- Provide enough detail for the interviewer to understand the complexity of the situation.

Example: "Last year, when I was working as a customer service manager at XYZ Company, we experienced a sudden 50% increase in customer complaints following a new product launch."

Task:
- Explain your responsibility or role in the situation.
- What was expected of you?
- What goal were you working toward?

Example: "As the customer service manager, it was my responsibility to address this surge in complaints, improve customer satisfaction, and protect the company's reputation."

Action:
- Describe the specific actions you took to address the situation.
- Be detailed about the steps you took.
- Focus on your individual contribution, even if you worked as part of a team.
- Use "I" statements to clarify your personal role.

Example: "I took several immediate actions. First, I analyzed the complaints to identify common issues. Then, I coordinated with our product development team to create quick fixes for the most pressing problems. I also implemented a new training program for our customer service representatives to better handle these specific complaints. Additionally, I personally reached out to our most valuable customers to address their concerns."

Result:

- Explain the outcomes of your actions.
- Quantify your results whenever possible.
- Even if the overall outcome was not ideal, focus on what you learned or how you grew from the experience.

Example: "As a result of these actions, we saw a 70% decrease in customer complaints within a month. Customer satisfaction scores improved by 25%, and we retained 95% of our most valuable customers. The product development team used the feedback to make significant improvements in the next product iteration. This experience taught me the importance of quick, data-driven decision-making and cross-departmental collaboration in crisis situations."

Tips for Using the STAR Method Effectively:

1. Prepare Multiple Stories: Have at least 5-7 stories prepared that showcase different skills and situations.

2. Be Concise: Aim to keep your STAR response to 2-3 minutes. Practice trimming unnecessary details.

3. Be Specific: Use concrete details and metrics to make your story more impactful and believable.

4. Show Growth: Even if the situation had challenges, focus on what you learned and how you've grown from the experience.

5. Tailor Your Stories: Choose stories that are most relevant to the job you're applying for.

6. Practice, But Don't Memorize: While it's good to practice your stories, avoid memorizing them word-for-word to keep your responses natural and adaptable.

7. Listen Carefully: Make sure your story actually answers the question asked. It's okay to ask for clarification if you're unsure.

8. Be Honest: While you want to present yourself in the best light, never fabricate or exaggerate your stories. Authenticity is key.

9. Emphasize Your Role: Even if it was a team effort, focus on your specific contributions and decision-making process.

10. Connect to the Future: If possible, conclude by relating how this experience has prepared you for the role you're interviewing for.

By mastering common interview questions, crafting compelling stories, and using the STAR method effectively, you'll be well-prepared to showcase your skills and experiences in a clear, engaging, and impactful way during your interview. Remember, the key is to practice these techniques until they feel natural, allowing you to present your best self with confidence and authenticity.

Advanced Interview Techniques

As you progress in your career or apply for more specialized roles, you may encounter more complex interview formats. These advanced techniques are designed to assess your skills, problem-solving abilities, and cultural fit in greater depth. In this chapter, we'll explore four common advanced interview techniques and provide strategies for excelling in each.

6.1 Behavioral Interviews: Predicting Future Performance

Behavioral interviews are based on the premise that past behavior is the best predictor of future performance. In these interviews, you'll be asked to provide specific examples of how you've handled situations in the past.

Key Characteristics:
   - Questions often start with phrases like "Tell me about a time when…" or "Give me an example of…"
   - Focus on real experiences rather than hypothetical situations
   - Require detailed, specific answers

Strategies for Success:

1. Use the STAR Method:
   - Situation: Describe the context
   - Task: Explain your responsibility

- Action: Detail the steps you took
  - Result: Share the outcome and what you learned

2. Prepare a Range of Examples:
  - Have stories ready that demonstrate key skills like leadership, teamwork, problem-solving, and adaptability
  - Ensure your examples are recent and relevant to the job you're applying for

3. Be Specific:
  - Provide concrete details about the situation, your actions, and the results
  - Use metrics where possible to quantify your achievements

4. Show Growth:
  - Even if the outcome wasn't ideal, explain what you learned and how you've applied that knowledge since

5. Practice Active Listening:
  - Make sure you understand the question before answering
  - It's okay to ask for clarification if needed

6. Be Honest:
  - Don't embellish or fabricate stories
  - If you don't have an example for a specific situation, explain how you would handle it based on related experiences

7. Tailor Your Responses:
  - Research the company and role to understand what skills and qualities they value most
  - Choose examples that highlight these specific attributes

Example Question and Response:
  Q: "Tell me about a time when you had to deal with a difficult team member."

A: "In my previous role as a project manager at XYZ Corp, we were working on a critical product launch (Situation). As the team lead, it was my responsibility to ensure all team members were contributing effectively (Task). One team member consistently missed deadlines and was often defensive when given feedback. I scheduled a private meeting with them to understand the root of the problem. It turned out they were struggling with some of the technical aspects of their role. I paired them with a more experienced team member for mentoring and adjusted their deadlines slightly to allow for this extra training (Action). As a result, their performance improved significantly over the next month. They met all subsequent deadlines, and the product launched successfully. This experience taught me the importance of addressing issues promptly and finding constructive solutions rather than just criticizing (Result)."

6.2 Case Interviews: Problem-Solving Under Pressure

Case interviews are common in consulting, finance, and some tech roles. They present you with a business problem or scenario and ask you to analyze it and provide recommendations.

Key Characteristics:
  - Often based on real business situations
  - Test your analytical, problem-solving, and communication skills
  - May involve numerical calculations or estimations

Strategies for Success:

1. Understand the Framework:
  - Familiarize yourself with common business frameworks (e.g., SWOT analysis, Porter's Five Forces)
  - Practice applying these frameworks to various business scenarios

2. Ask Clarifying Questions:

- Don't be afraid to ask for more information or clarification
- This shows engagement and ensures you understand the problem fully

3. Structure Your Approach:
   - Outline your approach before diving into the analysis
   - Break the problem down into manageable parts

4. Think Aloud:
   - Share your thought process as you work through the problem
   - This allows the interviewer to follow your reasoning and provide guidance if needed

5. Use Data Wisely:
   - If given data, use it to support your arguments
   - Be prepared to make reasonable estimates if exact figures aren't provided

6. Be Adaptable:
   - Be ready to change your approach if new information is introduced
   - Show that you can think on your feet

7. Provide a Clear Recommendation:
   - Summarize your findings and provide a clear, actionable recommendation
   - Be prepared to defend your recommendation if challenged

Example Case Question and Approach:

Q: "Our client is a large coffee shop chain considering expanding into the tea market. What factors should they consider, and would you recommend this expansion?"

Approach:
1. Clarify the objective: "Before we begin, I'd like to confirm that the main goal is to evaluate the potential for successful expansion into the tea market. Is that correct?"

2. Structure the analysis:
   "I'd like to approach this by considering four key areas:
   a) Market analysis: Size, growth, and trends in the tea market
   b) Competition: Existing players and barriers to entry
   c) Company capabilities: How well the client's existing resources and skills align with tea market needs
   d) Financial implications: Potential revenues, costs, and profitability"

3. Analyze each area, thinking aloud and asking for any available data.

4. Summarize findings and make a recommendation:
   "Based on our analysis, I would cautiously recommend proceeding with the expansion. The tea market is growing, particularly in the premium segment, which aligns well with our client's brand. While there are established competitors, our client's existing infrastructure and customer base provide significant advantages. However, I would recommend a phased approach, perhaps starting with a limited tea menu in existing stores to test the market before considering dedicated tea shops."

6.3 Technical Interviews: Demonstrating Expertise

Technical interviews are common in fields like engineering, IT, and data science. They assess your technical knowledge and problem-solving skills related to the specific role.

Key Characteristics:
   - May involve coding challenges, system design questions, or technical discussions
   - Often focus on fundamental concepts as well as specific technologies
   - May include both theoretical and practical components

Strategies for Success:

1. Review Fundamentals:
   - Brush up on core concepts in your field, even if you don't use them daily
   - Be prepared to explain basic principles clearly

2. Practice Coding:
   - If applicable, practice coding problems on platforms like LeetCode or HackerRank
   - Focus on writing clean, efficient code

3. Think Aloud:
   - Explain your thought process as you work through problems
   - This shows your problem-solving approach and allows the interviewer to provide hints if needed

4. Ask Clarifying Questions:
   - Ensure you understand the problem fully before starting
   - Don't hesitate to ask for more details or clarification

5. Consider Edge Cases:
   - Think about potential edge cases or unusual scenarios
   - Demonstrate your ability to consider all aspects of a problem

6. Be Honest About What You Don't Know:
   - If you're unsure about something, say so
   - Explain how you would go about finding the answer

7. Relate to Real-World Applications:
   - Where possible, connect technical concepts to practical applications
   - This demonstrates your understanding of how technology solves business problems

Example Technical Question and Approach:
   Q: "Design a system to handle millions of sensor readings per second from

IoT devices."

Approach:
1. Clarify requirements: "Before we start, could you provide more details about the type of sensor data, the required latency for processing, and any specific analytics needs?"

2. Outline high-level architecture:
   "I'd propose a system with these main components:
   a) Data ingestion layer using a distributed streaming platform like Apache Kafka
   b) Stream processing layer using a technology like Apache Flink or Spark Streaming
   c) Storage layer, possibly using a combination of a time-series database for recent data and cloud storage for historical data
   d) API layer for data access and integration with other systems"

3. Discuss each component in detail, explaining design choices and trade-offs.

4. Address scalability and fault tolerance:
   "To handle millions of readings per second, we'd need to ensure our system is horizontally scalable. We can achieve this by…"

5. Conclude with potential optimizations and areas for further discussion.

6.4 Panel Interviews: Engaging Multiple Interviewers

Panel interviews involve meeting with several interviewers simultaneously. They're often used to save time and to get different perspectives on a candidate.

Key Characteristics:
   - Multiple interviewers, often from different departments or levels of the

organization
- Can be more stressful due to the number of people involved
- May involve a mix of question types

Strategies for Success:

1. Research the Panel:
   - If possible, find out who will be on the panel and their roles
   - Tailor some of your questions and examples to their specific areas of expertise

2. Make Eye Contact with Everyone:
   - When answering a question, make eye contact with the person who asked it, but also glance at other panel members
   - This helps you engage with the entire group

3. Remember Names:
   - Try to remember and use the names of the panel members
   - This personalizes your responses and shows attention to detail

4. Be Consistent:
   - Your answers should be consistent regardless of who asks the question
   - Panel members may compare notes, so contradictions could raise red flags

5. Handle Cross-Talk Gracefully:
   - If panel members disagree or discuss something among themselves, wait patiently
   - If asked for your opinion on a disagreement, be diplomatic and show you can see multiple perspectives

6. Prepare Extra Examples:
   - With multiple interviewers, you may need more examples than in a one-

on-one interview
   - Have a broad range of stories ready to illustrate your skills and experiences

7. Manage Your Energy:
   - Panel interviews can be lengthy and draining
   - Pace yourself and maintain your energy throughout the interview

8. Follow Up Individually:
   - If possible, send individual thank-you notes to each panel member
   - Personalize each note based on your interactions during the interview

Example Approach:
"Good morning everyone. Thank you for taking the time to meet with me today. I'm excited to learn more about the role and how my experience might benefit your team.

[After introductions]

To answer your question, Mr. Johnson, about my experience with cross-functional projects..."

[Making eye contact with Mr. Johnson, but also glancing at other panel members]

"...Does that align with the type of projects your team typically handles, Ms. Garcia?"

[Directing a follow-up question to another panel member to engage them in the conversation]

By mastering these advanced interview techniques, you'll be well-prepared for a wide range of interview scenarios. Remember, the key to success in any interview format is thorough preparation, clear communication, and the ability to stay calm under pressure. Practice these techniques, and you'll be ready to showcase your skills and experience effectively, no matter what type of interview you face.

The Power of Questions: What to Ask Your Interviewer

Asking thoughtful, insightful questions during an interview is not just about gathering information—it's an opportunity to demonstrate your interest, intelligence, and fit for the role. Well-crafted questions can set you apart from other candidates and provide valuable insights into the company and position. This chapter will guide you through formulating powerful questions that showcase your value, help you understand the company culture, and position you as a forward-thinking candidate.

7.1 Questions That Demonstrate Your Value

These questions show that you're already thinking about how you can contribute to the company's success. They demonstrate your enthusiasm, preparation, and strategic thinking.

1. "In the first 90 days, what would you consider to be the most important priorities for this role?"

Why it's powerful: This question shows that you're action-oriented and eager to make an impact. It also gives you insight into the immediate challenges you'd face if hired.

2. "What specific skills or experiences do you think would make someone particularly successful in this position?"

Why it's powerful: This allows you to highlight how your background aligns with what they're seeking, even if you haven't had the chance to do so earlier in the interview.

3. "Can you tell me about a project or initiative where someone in this role made a significant impact?"

Why it's powerful: This question demonstrates your interest in making meaningful contributions. It also provides you with an example of what success looks like in this role.

4. "What are the biggest challenges facing the team/department right now, and how could someone in this role help address them?"

Why it's powerful: This shows that you're thinking about the broader context of the role and how you can add value beyond the basic job description.

5. "How does this role contribute to the overall goals of the department/company?"

Why it's powerful: This question demonstrates your strategic thinking and desire to align your work with larger organizational objectives.

6. "Are there any areas where you feel the team could improve its processes or efficiency?"

Why it's powerful: This shows your problem-solving mindset and eagerness to contribute to team improvement.

7. "What opportunities for professional development or growth does this role offer?"

Why it's powerful: This question shows your commitment to long-term growth and adding increasing value to the company over time.

8. "How do you measure success for this position?"
Why it's powerful: This demonstrates your results-oriented mindset and desire to meet or exceed expectations.

9. "Can you tell me about a time when someone in this role encountered a significant challenge? How did they overcome it?"
Why it's powerful: This shows your interest in understanding and preparing for potential challenges, as well as your problem-solving orientation.

10. "What skills or experiences do you think will become increasingly important for this role in the next 2-3 years?"
Why it's powerful: This question demonstrates your forward-thinking approach and commitment to staying relevant in a changing business environment.

7.2 Questions That Reveal Company Culture

Understanding company culture is crucial for determining whether you'll thrive in a particular work environment. These questions can help you gauge the company's values, work style, and employee experience.

1. "How would you describe the company's culture in three words?"
Why it's powerful: This forces the interviewer to distill the culture into its essence, giving you a quick snapshot of what to expect.

2. "What do you enjoy most about working here?"
Why it's powerful: This personal question can provide genuine insights into the positive aspects of the company culture.

3. "How does the company support work-life balance?"
Why it's powerful: This question addresses an important aspect of company culture without making assumptions about specific policies.

4. "Can you tell me about a recent company-wide initiative that exemplified the company's values?"
   Why it's powerful: This question reveals how the company puts its stated values into practice.

5. "How does the company foster innovation and creativity?"
   Why it's powerful: This question helps you understand if the company culture encourages new ideas and approaches.

6. "What types of people tend to be most successful here?"
   Why it's powerful: The answer to this can reveal a lot about the traits and behaviors that are valued in the company culture.

7. "How does the company approach professional development and learning?"
   Why it's powerful: This question shows your interest in growth while revealing the company's commitment to employee development.

8. "Can you tell me about the last company event or celebration?"
   Why it's powerful: This can provide insights into how the company builds community and recognizes achievements.

9. "How would you describe the leadership style of the senior management team?"
   Why it's powerful: This can give you a sense of the overall management approach and how it impacts company culture.

10. "What's the most common piece of feedback you receive from employees about working here?"
    Why it's powerful: This can reveal both positive aspects and potential areas of improvement in the company culture.

11. "How does the company handle disagreements or conflicts?"
    Why it's powerful: This question can provide insights into the company's

communication style and problem-solving approach.

12. "Can you tell me about a time when an employee suggested a major change? How was it received?"
   Why it's powerful: This can reveal how open the company is to new ideas and how it values employee input.

7.3 Questions That Position You as a Forward-Thinker

These questions demonstrate your strategic thinking and long-term perspective. They show that you're not just interested in the job, but in the future of the company and industry.

1. "What do you see as the biggest opportunities for the company in the next 3-5 years?"
   Why it's powerful: This shows you're thinking about the company's future and how you might contribute to its long-term success.

2. "How is the company preparing for [specific industry trend or challenge]?"
   Why it's powerful: This demonstrates your awareness of industry trends and your interest in how the company is positioning itself for the future.

3. "What emerging technologies do you think will have the biggest impact on this role/industry in the coming years?"
   Why it's powerful: This question showcases your technological awareness and interest in staying ahead of the curve.

4. "How does the company approach innovation and stay competitive in a rapidly changing market?"
   Why it's powerful: This demonstrates your understanding of the importance of innovation and adaptability in today's business environment.

5. "What potential changes in the regulatory environment do you foresee

impacting the company, and how is the company preparing for these?"

Why it's powerful: This shows your awareness of external factors that could affect the business and your interest in strategic planning.

6. "How is the company addressing sustainability and corporate social responsibility?"

Why it's powerful: This question demonstrates your awareness of the growing importance of these issues in the business world.

7. "What skills do you think will be most crucial for this role in the next 5-10 years?"

Why it's powerful: This shows your commitment to long-term career development and aligning your skills with future needs.

8. "How is the company adapting its strategies in response to [recent industry development or market shift]?"

Why it's powerful: This demonstrates your up-to-date knowledge of the industry and interest in strategic adaptation.

9. "What potential disruptions to the industry are you most concerned about, and how is the company positioning itself to handle these?"

Why it's powerful: This question shows your ability to think critically about potential challenges and your interest in the company's strategic response.

10. "How does the company envision its market position evolving over the next decade?"

Why it's powerful: This demonstrates your interest in the long-term vision of the company and how your role might contribute to that vision.

11. "What initiatives is the company taking to attract and retain top talent in an increasingly competitive job market?"

Why it's powerful: This shows your awareness of broader employment trends and your interest in the company's human capital strategy.

THE POWER OF QUESTIONS: WHAT TO ASK YOUR INTERVIEWER

12. "How is the company leveraging data and analytics to drive decision-making and strategy?"

Why it's powerful: This demonstrates your understanding of the importance of data in modern business and your interest in data-driven approaches.

Tips for Asking Questions Effectively:

1. Timing: Save most of your questions for the end of the interview when you're typically invited to ask them. However, if appropriate opportunities arise during the conversation, don't be afraid to ask relevant questions.

2. Quantity: Prepare more questions than you think you'll need. Aim for at least 5-7, as some may be answered during the course of the interview.

3. Relevance: Tailor your questions to the specific role and company. Generic questions can make you appear unprepared or uninterested.

4. Listen Actively: Pay attention to the answers you receive. They may inspire follow-up questions that show you're engaged in the conversation.

5. Avoid Sensitive Topics: In the initial interviews, it's generally best to avoid questions about salary, benefits, or time off unless the interviewer brings them up.

6. Show Genuine Interest: Your tone and body language should convey sincere curiosity. These questions are not just for show, but to help you make an informed decision about the role.

7. Take Notes: Jot down key points from the answers. This shows you're attentive and provides you with valuable information for follow-up communications or future interview rounds.

8. Thank the Interviewer: After they've answered your questions, thank

them for their insights. This courtesy can leave a positive final impression.

Remember, the questions you ask can be just as important as the answers you give in an interview. They provide an opportunity to demonstrate your preparation, enthusiasm, and strategic thinking. By asking thoughtful questions that showcase your value, probe the company culture, and position you as a forward-thinker, you'll leave a lasting positive impression and gain valuable insights to help you make an informed decision about the role.

Navigating Difficult Interview Scenarios

Even with thorough preparation, you may encounter challenging situations during an interview. How you handle these moments can significantly impact the outcome of your interview. This chapter will guide you through some common difficult scenarios and provide strategies for navigating them successfully.

8.1 Addressing Employment Gaps and Job Hopping

Employment gaps and a history of frequent job changes can raise red flags for potential employers. However, with the right approach, you can address these concerns effectively.

Addressing Employment Gaps:

1. Be Honest: Never try to hide or lie about employment gaps. Honesty is crucial for building trust with potential employers.

2. Provide Context: Briefly explain the reason for the gap. Common reasons include:
    - Further education or training
    - Family responsibilities (e.g., caring for a child or elderly parent)
    - Health issues (now resolved)
    - Volunteer work or personal projects

3. Focus on Productive Activities: Highlight any relevant activities you engaged in during the gap:
   - "During that time, I completed an online course in digital marketing to enhance my skills."
   - "I volunteered with a local non-profit, which improved my project management abilities."

4. Emphasize Your Current Readiness: Make it clear that you're now fully prepared to commit to the role.

5. Keep it Concise: Provide a brief, clear explanation without oversharing personal details.

Example Response:
"Yes, there was a gap in my employment from 2019 to 2020. During that time, I took a step back to care for an ill family member. While it was challenging, I used some of that time to complete an online certification in project management. This experience not only enhanced my skills but also reinforced my ability to manage multiple priorities effectively. I'm now fully available and eager to apply these skills in a professional setting."

Addressing Job Hopping:

1. Highlight Growth and Learning: Frame each job change as a step towards your career goals.

2. Emphasize Valuable Experiences: Discuss how each role contributed to your skill set and industry knowledge.

3. Show Loyalty Where Possible: If you have any longer tenures, make sure to point them out.

4. Address It Proactively: If you know it's a concern, bring it up yourself and

explain your career path.

5. Express Commitment: Emphasize your desire for a long-term role where you can grow and contribute.

Example Response:
"I understand my resume shows several job changes in recent years. Each move was a strategic decision to gain diverse experience and broaden my skill set in different aspects of marketing. For example, at Company A, I focused on digital marketing strategies, while at Company B, I honed my skills in content creation and SEO. Now, I'm looking for a role where I can bring together all these skills and commit to a long-term position. Your company's focus on integrated marketing strategies aligns perfectly with my career goals."

8.2 Discussing Salary Expectations Strategically

Salary discussions can be tricky to navigate. Here's how to approach them:

1. Do Your Research: Before the interview, research salary ranges for similar positions in your industry and location. Websites like Glassdoor, Payscale, and industry-specific salary surveys can be helpful.

2. Delay the Discussion if Possible: If asked about salary expectations early in the process, try to politely defer the conversation:
"I'd like to learn more about the role and your expectations before discussing compensation. Can we revisit this topic once we've determined I'm a good fit for the position?"

3. Provide a Range: When you do discuss numbers, give a range rather than a specific figure. This allows for negotiation:
"Based on my research and experience, I'm looking for a salary in the range of $X to $Y. However, I'm open to discussion based on the total compensation

package."

4. Consider the Total Package: Remember that salary is just one part of compensation. Be prepared to discuss benefits, bonuses, stock options, and other perks.

5. Flip the Question: You can ask about the budgeted range for the role:
   "To ensure we're on the same page, could you share the salary range you've budgeted for this position?"

6. Emphasize Value: When discussing salary, reinforce the value you'll bring to the role:
   "Given my track record of increasing sales by 20% in my previous role, I believe a salary in the range of $X to $Y would be appropriate. I'm excited about the opportunity to bring similar results to your team."

7. Be Prepared to Negotiate: If the offered salary is lower than expected, be prepared to negotiate professionally:
   "While I'm very excited about the opportunity, the offer is a bit below my expectations given my experience and the market rate. Is there room for discussion on this?"

Remember, the goal is to find a mutually beneficial arrangement. Be professional, flexible, and focus on the value you can bring to the role.

8.3 Overcoming Lack of Experience or Qualifications

If you're changing careers or applying for a role where you don't meet all the stated qualifications, you may need to address this during the interview.

1. Focus on Transferable Skills: Identify skills from your past experiences that apply to the new role:
   "While I haven't worked directly in marketing, my experience in customer

service has honed my communication skills and ability to understand consumer needs, which are crucial in creating effective marketing strategies."

2. Highlight Relevant Projects or Volunteer Work: Even if not from paid work, these can demonstrate applicable skills:

"Although I'm new to professional project management, I successfully coordinated a major fundraising event for a local nonprofit, managing timelines, budgets, and a team of volunteers."

3. Emphasize Your Learning Ability: Show that you're quick to learn and adapt:

"I'm a fast learner and have consistently picked up new skills quickly in my previous roles. I'm confident I can quickly get up to speed on the specific technologies used in this position."

4. Show Enthusiasm and Commitment: Your passion for the role can sometimes outweigh lack of experience:

"What I might lack in direct experience, I make up for in enthusiasm and commitment. I've been following developments in this field closely and am dedicated to building a career in this area."

5. Provide Examples of Overcoming Challenges: Demonstrate your problem-solving skills:

"In my previous role, I was initially unfamiliar with the CRM system. I took online courses in my free time and within a month, I was assisting colleagues with the software."

6. Address the Issue Directly: Don't try to hide your lack of experience. Instead, address it openly and positively:

"I understand I may not have the typical background for this role. However, I believe my unique perspective, combined with my strong analytical skills and eagerness to learn, will allow me to bring fresh ideas to the team."

7. Offer to Prove Yourself: If appropriate, suggest a trial period or project: "I'm confident in my ability to excel in this role. If you have any concerns, I'd be open to starting with a trial project to demonstrate my capabilities."

Remember, many skills can be taught, but qualities like enthusiasm, adaptability, and a strong work ethic are often more valuable to employers in the long run.

8.4 Handling Unexpected or Inappropriate Questions

Sometimes, you might be asked questions that catch you off guard or seem inappropriate. Here's how to handle these situations:

1. Illegal Questions: Some questions about age, race, religion, marital status, or sexual orientation are illegal in many jurisdictions. If asked such a question:
   - Politely deflect: "I'm not comfortable answering that question. Could we instead discuss my qualifications for the role?"
   - Address the underlying concern: If you think there's a legitimate concern behind the question, address that instead. For example, if asked about children, you might say: "If you're concerned about my availability, I can assure you that I'm fully committed to the responsibilities of this role."

2. Overly Personal Questions: For questions that feel too personal but aren't necessarily illegal:
   - Redirect to professional relevance: "I prefer to keep my personal and professional lives separate. However, I can tell you about my professional experiences that relate to this role."

3. Surprise Technical Questions: If you're asked a technical question you're not prepared for:
   - Stay calm and think out loud: "That's an interesting question. Let me think through this…"
   - If you don't know the answer, be honest but show your problem-solving

approach: "I'm not immediately familiar with that specific technology, but here's how I would approach learning about it..."

4. Behavioral Questions You Didn't Prepare For: If asked about a situation you didn't anticipate:
   - Take a moment to think: "That's a great question. Let me think of the best example..."
   - If you can't think of a perfect fit, use a similar situation: "While I haven't encountered that exact situation, I did face a similar challenge when..."

5. Questions About Competitors: If asked about other companies you're interviewing with:
   - Be honest but discreet: "I'm exploring several opportunities in the [industry/field], but this role at your company is particularly exciting to me because..."

6. Brainteaser Questions: Some companies ask unusual questions to see how you think. For these:
   - Think out loud: Show your problem-solving process.
   - Stay calm and approach it logically: Break the problem down into smaller parts.
   - It's okay to ask for clarification or more information.

7. Negative Questions About Previous Employers: If asked why you're leaving your current job or about problems with previous employers:
   - Stay positive: Focus on what you're moving towards, not what you're leaving behind.
   - Be diplomatic: "While I've learned a lot in my current role, I'm looking for new challenges that align with my career goals."

8. Questions About Gaps in Employment: We covered this earlier, but remember to be honest and focus on any productive activities during that time.

General Tips for Handling Difficult Questions:

1. Stay Calm: Your composure under pressure is often more important than the specific answer you give.

2. Buy Time If Needed: It's okay to say, "That's an interesting question. Let me think about that for a moment."

3. Be Honest: If you don't know something, admit it, but explain how you would find the answer.

4. Redirect: If a question seems irrelevant, try to steer the conversation back to your qualifications for the role.

5. Prepare: While you can't anticipate every question, thorough preparation can help you handle unexpected queries more confidently.

6. Follow Up: If you feel you handled a question poorly, you can address it in your thank-you email after the interview.

Remember, how you handle difficult scenarios can actually become a strength. Demonstrating grace under pressure, honesty, and problem-solving skills when faced with challenging questions can leave a positive impression on interviewers. Your ability to navigate these situations professionally can set you apart from other candidates and showcase valuable soft skills that are crucial in any workplace.

The Digital Interview: Mastering Video and Phone Interviews

In today's increasingly digital world, video and phone interviews have become commonplace. These remote interview formats present unique challenges and opportunities. Mastering them is essential for modern job seekers. This chapter will guide you through the process of acing digital interviews, from setting up your space to projecting confidence through the screen.

9.1 Setting Up Your Space for Success

Your environment plays a crucial role in the success of your digital interview. Here's how to create an ideal setting:

1. Choose the Right Location:
   - Select a quiet room with minimal background noise.
   - Ensure good lighting, preferably natural light from a window in front of you.
   - If natural light isn't available, use soft, diffused lighting to avoid harsh shadows.

2. Prepare Your Background:
   - Opt for a clean, professional background. A plain wall or organized bookshelf works well.

- Avoid busy or distracting backgrounds.
  - If using a virtual background, choose something subtle and professional.

3. Position Your Camera:
  - Place your camera at eye level. This might mean elevating your laptop on a stack of books.
  - Sit at arm's length from the camera.
  - Ensure your head and shoulders are fully in frame.

4. Check Your Audio:
  - Use a good quality microphone. Your computer's built-in mic might not be sufficient.
  - Test your audio beforehand to ensure clear sound without echo.

5. Minimize Distractions:
  - Turn off notifications on your computer and phone.
  - If at home, inform family members or roommates about your interview to ensure quiet.
  - Keep pets in another room to avoid unexpected interruptions.

6. Prepare Your Materials:
  - Have a copy of your resume, the job description, and any notes within easy reach.
  - Keep a glass of water nearby in case your throat gets dry.

7. Dress Professionally:
  - Dress as you would for an in-person interview, including appropriate bottoms (in case you need to stand up).
  - Avoid bright patterns or colors that might be distracting on camera.

8. Control the Temperature:
  - Ensure the room is at a comfortable temperature to avoid sweating or shivering during the interview.

9. Have a Backup Plan:
   - Be prepared with a phone number to call in case of technical difficulties with the video.

10. Practice in Your Space:
    - Do a trial run in your chosen location to identify and address any issues.

For Phone Interviews:
   - Choose a location with excellent cell reception or use a landline if possible.
   - Use headphones to keep your hands free for taking notes.
   - Have all necessary documents spread out in front of you for easy reference.

9.2 Technology Tips to Avoid Common Pitfalls

Technical issues can derail an otherwise great interview. Here's how to avoid common technology pitfalls:

1. Test Your Equipment:
   - Do a test call with a friend to check your video and audio quality.
   - Familiarize yourself with the video conferencing platform (Zoom, Skype, Google Meet, etc.) beforehand.

2. Ensure a Strong Internet Connection:
   - If possible, use a wired ethernet connection instead of Wi-Fi for more stability.
   - Close unnecessary browser tabs and applications to free up bandwidth.
   - Have a backup internet source (like your phone's hotspot) ready in case of connection issues.

3. Update Your Software:
   - Ensure your operating system and video conferencing software are up-to-date.
   - Run any necessary updates well before the interview to avoid last-minute

delays.

4. Charge Your Devices:
    - Ensure your computer or phone is fully charged.
    - Keep your charger nearby as a precaution.

5. Use the Right Name and Profile Picture:
    - Set your display name to your full name.
    - Use a professional profile picture if required by the platform.

6. Master the Mute Button:
    - Know how to quickly mute and unmute yourself.
    - Stay muted when not speaking to minimize background noise.

7. Look at the Camera:
    - Position the video window near your camera to maintain eye contact.
    - Resist the urge to watch yourself on the screen.

8. Be Prepared for Screen Sharing:
    - Close any unnecessary or personal windows on your computer.
    - Have any documents or presentations you might need to share ready and easily accessible.

9. Have a Tech Troubleshooting Plan:
    - Know how to quickly switch to phone if video fails.
    - Have the interviewer's contact information readily available.

10. Optimize Video Settings:
    - Learn how to adjust video settings like brightness and contrast for the best image quality.

11. Use Good Headphones:
    - Quality headphones can significantly improve audio clarity and reduce

echo.

12. Disable Notifications:
   - Turn off all notifications on your device to avoid distracting pings or pop-ups during the interview.

For Phone Interviews:
   - Use a reliable phone with good call quality.
   - If using a cell phone, ensure it's fully charged and you're in an area with strong signal.
   - Consider using a hands-free option to allow for easy note-taking.

9.3 Projecting Confidence Through the Screen

Conveying confidence and building rapport can be challenging in a digital format. Here's how to project confidence effectively:

1. Make Eye Contact:
   - Look directly into the camera when speaking, not at the screen.
   - This creates the illusion of eye contact for the interviewer.

2. Use Appropriate Body Language:
   - Sit up straight with your shoulders back.
   - Lean slightly forward to show engagement.
   - Use natural hand gestures, keeping them in frame.

3. Smile and Show Enthusiasm:
   - Smile naturally throughout the conversation.
   - Show genuine interest through your facial expressions and tone of voice.

4. Speak Clearly and at a Moderate Pace:
   - Enunciate your words clearly to compensate for potential audio issues.
   - Pause briefly after making key points to ensure clarity.

5. Use Active Listening Cues:
   - Nod and use small verbal affirmations (like "I see" or "mm-hmm") to show you're engaged.
   - Be careful not to interrupt, as lag can make timing more challenging.

6. Maintain a Confident Tone:
   - Speak with conviction and avoid upward inflections that can make statements sound like questions.
   - Use a slightly lower pitch, which often conveys authority.

7. Practice Virtual Presence:
   - Record yourself in mock interviews to identify areas for improvement in your virtual presence.
   - Pay attention to your posture, facial expressions, and vocal tone.

8. Dress for Confidence:
   - Wear clothes that make you feel confident and professional.
   - Avoid busy patterns or bright colors that might be distracting on camera.

9. Be Prepared:
   - Having notes and materials organized will help you feel more confident.
   - Practice your responses to common questions in the digital format.

10. Manage Your Energy:
    - Digital interviews can be draining. Take deep breaths and stay hydrated.
    - If you have multiple interviews, schedule breaks in between to recharge.

11. Use Notes Strategically:
    - It's okay to have notes, but don't rely on them too heavily.
    - Glance at them naturally without breaking eye contact for long periods.

12. Handle Technical Issues Gracefully:
    - If you encounter problems, stay calm and professional.

- How you handle unexpected issues can demonstrate your problem-solving skills and adaptability.

13. End on a Strong Note:
    - Thank the interviewer for their time.
    - Express your continued interest in the position and the company.

For Phone Interviews:
   - Stand up and walk around if it helps you feel more energetic and confident.
   - Smile while you speak – it affects the tone of your voice positively.
   - Use verbal cues to convey your engagement, as the interviewer can't see your body language.

Additional Tips for Digital Interview Success:

1. Practice with the Technology:
   - Conduct mock interviews using the same technology to get comfortable with the format.
   - Ask a friend to give you feedback on your virtual presence.

2. Be Early:
   - Log in to the video call 5-10 minutes early to address any last-minute technical issues.

3. Have a Glass of Water Nearby:
   - Stay hydrated, but be careful not to spill on your equipment.

4. Use the Chat Function Wisely:
   - If there's a chat function, use it to share links or information if appropriate, but don't let it distract you from the conversation.

5. Follow Up Appropriately:
   - Send a thank-you email within 24 hours, referencing specific points from

your conversation.

6. Be Flexible:
   - Be prepared to adapt if the interviewer suggests switching from video to phone or vice versa.

7. Consider Your Time Zone:
   - If interviewing across time zones, double-check the interview time to avoid confusion.

8. Minimize Awkward Silences:
   - In case of lag, wait a beat before speaking to ensure the interviewer has finished their thought.

9. Use Physical Cues:
   - If you need a moment to think, use physical cues like nodding to show you're engaged and processing the question.

10. Be Authentic:
    - While it's important to project confidence, don't forget to be yourself. Authenticity can shine through even in a digital format.

Mastering digital interviews is an essential skill in today's job market. By setting up your space effectively, managing technology smoothly, and projecting confidence through the screen, you can make a strong impression in video and phone interviews. Remember, the key is preparation and practice. The more comfortable you become with the digital interview format, the more your true qualifications and personality can shine through. With these strategies, you'll be well-equipped to ace your next digital interview and move forward in your career journey.

Interview Follow-Up: Sealing the Deal

The interview process doesn't end when you walk out of the room or log off from your video call. The follow-up phase is crucial in solidifying your candidacy and potentially securing a job offer. This chapter will guide you through the essential steps of post-interview follow-up, including crafting the perfect thank-you note, following up appropriately, and negotiating job offers effectively.

10.1 The Art of the Thank-You Note

Sending a thank-you note after an interview is not just a courtesy; it's a strategic move that can set you apart from other candidates and reinforce your interest in the position.

Key Elements of an Effective Thank-You Note:

1. Timeliness:
   - Send your thank-you note within 24 hours of the interview.
   - This shows enthusiasm and keeps you fresh in the interviewer's mind.

2. Personalization:
   - Address the interviewer by name.
   - Reference specific topics discussed during the interview.

3. Gratitude:

- Express sincere appreciation for the interviewer's time and the opportunity.

4. Reiterate Interest:
   - Confirm your enthusiasm for the position and the company.

5. Reinforce Key Points:
   - Briefly remind the interviewer of your relevant skills and experiences.

6. Add Value:
   - Include any additional information that supports your candidacy.

7. Professionalism:
   - Use a professional tone and format.
   - Proofread carefully to avoid any errors.

8. Conciseness:
   - Keep the note brief – typically no more than a few paragraphs.

Sample Thank-You Note:

Subject: Thank You for the [Position] Interview

Dear [Interviewer's Name],

Thank you for taking the time to meet with me yesterday regarding the [Position] role at [Company Name]. I enjoyed our conversation and am even more excited about the opportunity to join your team.

Your description of the challenges facing the marketing department, particularly in expanding your digital presence, aligns perfectly with my experience. As I mentioned, in my previous role at [Previous Company], I successfully led a digital transformation project that increased our online engagement by

50%. I'm confident I can bring similar results to [Company Name].

I was also impressed by [Company Name]'s commitment to innovation and sustainability, as evidenced by your recent [specific initiative or project]. This aligns well with my personal values and professional goals.

If you need any additional information, please don't hesitate to contact me. I look forward to hearing about the next steps in the process.

Thank you again for your time and consideration.

Best regards,
   [Your Name]

Tips for Thank-You Notes:

1. Email vs. Handwritten:
   - In most cases, an email is appropriate and ensures timely delivery.
   - For more traditional industries, a handwritten note can be a nice touch, but send an email as well to ensure timeliness.

2. Multiple Interviewers:
   - Send individual notes to each person you met with.
   - Personalize each note with specific details from your conversation with that interviewer.

3. After a Phone Interview:
   - Even after a brief phone screening, send a short thank-you email.
   - Use this as an opportunity to reiterate your interest in moving forward in the process.

4. Follow-Up Materials:
   - If you discussed providing additional information or samples of your

work, include these with your thank-you note or reference when they can expect to receive them.

5. Tone:
   - Match the tone of your note to the company culture and your interaction with the interviewer.

6. Length:
   - Keep it concise. A few short paragraphs are usually sufficient.

10.2 Following Up Without Being Pushy

After sending your thank-you note, you may find yourself waiting to hear back about the next steps. Here's how to follow up effectively without coming across as pushy:

1. Respect the Timeline:
   - If the interviewer gave you a timeline for the next steps, wait until after that date to follow up.
   - If no timeline was provided, it's generally appropriate to follow up after one week.

2. Choose the Right Medium:
   - Email is usually the best method for follow-ups.
   - Use the same email chain as your thank-you note to keep all communication in one place.

3. Be Concise:
   - Keep your follow-up message brief and to the point.

4. Reiterate Your Interest:
   - Use this opportunity to reaffirm your enthusiasm for the position.

INTERVIEW FOLLOW-UP: SEALING THE DEAL

5. Offer Additional Information:
   - Ask if there's any other information you can provide to support your candidacy.

6. Be Patient:
   - Limit your follow-ups to once every 1-2 weeks unless told otherwise.

7. Know When to Move On:
   - If you don't hear back after 2-3 follow-ups, it may be time to focus your energy elsewhere.

Sample Follow-Up Email:

Subject: Following Up on [Position] Interview

Dear [Interviewer's Name],

I hope this email finds you well. I wanted to follow up on my interview for the [Position] role, which we discussed on [Interview Date]. I'm still very excited about the opportunity to join [Company Name] and contribute to [specific project or goal discussed].

I understand you're in the process of making a decision, and I was wondering if you could provide any updates on the timeline or if you need any additional information from me.

Thank you again for your time and consideration. I look forward to hearing from you.

Best regards,
   [Your Name]

10.3 Negotiating Job Offers Like a Pro

Receiving a job offer is exciting, but it's also the beginning of a crucial phase: negotiation. Here's how to navigate this process professionally and effectively:

1. Express Gratitude:
   - Thank the employer for the offer and express your enthusiasm.
   - Ask for the offer in writing if it wasn't initially provided.

2. Request Time to Consider:
   - It's perfectly acceptable to ask for time to review the offer.
   - Typically, 2-3 days is reasonable for most positions.

3. Evaluate the Entire Package:
   - Consider all aspects of the offer, including salary, benefits, work-life balance, growth opportunities, and company culture.

4. Research and Prepare:
   - Know your market value based on industry standards and your experience.
   - Prioritize what's most important to you in the offer.

5. Start with the Right Mindset:
   - Approach negotiations as a collaborative discussion, not a confrontation.
   - Remember that the company wants you; they've already invested time in the hiring process.

6. Focus on Value:
   - Frame your negotiation in terms of the value you bring to the company.
   - Use specific examples from your experience to justify your requests.

7. Be Specific:
   - Clearly articulate what you're asking for and why.
   - If asking for a higher salary, provide a specific number or range.

8. Consider Non-Salary Benefits:
   - If there's limited flexibility on salary, consider negotiating other benefits like additional vacation time, flexible working hours, or professional development opportunities.

9. Use Positive Language:
   - Frame your requests positively. Instead of "I need," try "Would you consider?"

10. Be Prepared to Compromise:
    - Know your walk-away point, but also be open to creative solutions.

11. Get it in Writing:
    - Once you've reached an agreement, make sure all changes are documented in a revised offer letter.

12. Maintain Professionalism:
    - Regardless of the outcome, remain professional and courteous throughout the process.

Sample Negotiation Script:

"Thank you for the offer. I'm excited about the opportunity to join [Company Name]. Based on my research and the value I believe I can bring to this role, particularly with my experience in [specific skill or achievement], I was hoping we could discuss the possibility of a salary in the range of [your desired range]. I'm also interested in discussing [specific benefit or opportunity]. Would you be open to exploring these adjustments?"

Tips for Successful Negotiation:

1. Practice Your Pitch:
   - Rehearse your negotiation points with a friend or mentor.

2. Consider the Entire Package:
   - Sometimes, benefits like stock options or bonuses can make up for a lower base salary.

3. Use Silence:
   - After making a request, resist the urge to fill silence. Let the other party respond.

4. Be Prepared to Explain Why:
   - Have clear, value-based reasons for each of your requests.

5. Don't Bluff:
   - Only mention other offers if they genuinely exist and you're seriously considering them.

6. Be Realistic:
   - While it's good to aim high, ensure your requests are within reasonable market ranges.

7. Consider Timing:
   - If possible, try to have all your requests addressed at once rather than in multiple rounds.

8. Stay Positive:
   - Even if negotiations become tense, maintain a positive, professional demeanor.

9. Get Support:
   - If you're unsure about any part of the offer, don't hesitate to seek advice from a mentor or career counselor.

10. Be Prepared to Walk Away:
    - If the final offer doesn't meet your minimum requirements, be prepared

to decline politely.

Closing the Deal:

Once you've reached an agreement:

1. Get the Final Offer in Writing:
   - Ensure all negotiated terms are included in the official offer letter.

2. Review Carefully:
   - Check all details, including start date, job title, and agreed-upon terms.

3. Formally Accept:
   - Send a formal acceptance email, expressing your enthusiasm to join the team.

4. Withdraw Other Applications:
   - If you've been interviewing elsewhere, professionally withdraw your candidacy from those positions.

5. Plan Your Transition:
   - If currently employed, prepare to give notice and ensure a smooth handover.

Remember, the post-interview phase is your final opportunity to solidify your candidacy and ensure that the potential job aligns with your career goals and expectations. By mastering the art of the thank-you note, following up appropriately, and negotiating skillfully, you significantly increase your chances of not just landing the job, but securing a role and compensation package that truly fits your needs and aspirations. Approach this phase with the same professionalism and preparation you brought to the interview itself, and you'll be well-positioned to start your new role on a positive note.

Industry-Specific Interview Guides

While many interview principles are universal, each industry has its unique focus areas and expectations. Understanding these nuances can give you a significant advantage in your interview preparation. This chapter provides tailored guidance for interviews in six major sectors: Tech and IT, Finance and Banking, Healthcare, Marketing and Creative Fields, Education, and the Non-Profit Sector.

11.1 Tech and IT

The tech industry is known for its fast-paced environment and constant innovation. Interviews in this sector often focus on technical skills, problem-solving abilities, and cultural fit.

Key Focus Areas:
1. Technical Skills: Expect in-depth questions about programming languages, frameworks, and methodologies relevant to the role.

2. Problem-Solving: Be prepared for coding challenges or technical puzzles.

3. System Design: For more senior roles, you may be asked to design a system or architecture.

4. Adaptability: Demonstrate your ability to learn new technologies quickly.

5. Teamwork: Highlight experiences working in agile environments or cross-functional teams.

Sample Questions:
- "Describe a complex technical problem you've solved recently. What was your approach?"
- "How would you design a scalable web application that can handle millions of users?"
- "What's your experience with cloud technologies like AWS or Azure?"

Tips:
- Stay updated on the latest industry trends and technologies.
- Practice coding on platforms like LeetCode or HackerRank.
- Be prepared to discuss your contributions to open-source projects or personal tech projects.
- Familiarize yourself with the company's products or services and be ready to discuss potential improvements.

11.2 Finance and Banking

The finance sector values precision, analytical skills, and a strong understanding of market dynamics. Interviews often assess your technical knowledge, ethical standards, and ability to work under pressure.

Key Focus Areas:
1. Technical Knowledge: Expect questions on financial models, valuation methods, and market analysis.

2. Regulatory Awareness: Demonstrate understanding of relevant financial regulations and compliance requirements.

3. Risk Management: Be prepared to discuss strategies for identifying and mitigating financial risks.

4. Analytical Skills: You may be given case studies or financial scenarios to analyze.

5. Ethical Standards: Be ready to discuss how you handle ethical dilemmas in financial decision-making.

Sample Questions:
   - "Walk me through a discounted cash flow (DCF) model. When might it not be an appropriate valuation method?"
   - "How would you explain the current state of the economy to a client?"
   - "Describe a situation where you had to make a difficult financial decision with limited information."

Tips:
   - Stay updated on current financial news and market trends.
   - Be prepared to discuss your views on economic outlook and market conditions.
   - Practice mental math and quick financial calculations.
   - Understand the specific area of finance the role focuses on (e.g., corporate finance, investment banking, risk management) and tailor your preparation accordingly.

11.3 Healthcare

Healthcare interviews often focus on a combination of technical knowledge, patient care skills, and understanding of healthcare systems and regulations.

Key Focus Areas:
   1. Clinical Knowledge: For clinical roles, expect in-depth questions about medical procedures, patient care protocols, and best practices.

2. Regulatory Compliance: Demonstrate understanding of healthcare laws and regulations (e.g., HIPAA in the US).

3. Patient Care: Highlight your approach to providing compassionate, effective patient care.

4. Teamwork: Emphasize experiences working in multidisciplinary healthcare teams.

5. Adaptability: Show how you stay updated with evolving medical knowledge and technologies.

Sample Questions:
   - "Describe a challenging patient interaction and how you handled it."
   - "How do you ensure patient confidentiality in your daily work?"
   - "What strategies do you use to stay updated with the latest medical research in your field?"

Tips:
   - Be prepared to discuss specific cases or scenarios relevant to your specialization.
   - Highlight any experience with electronic health records (EHR) systems.
   - Demonstrate your commitment to continuing education and professional development.
   - Be ready to discuss how you handle high-stress situations and maintain work-life balance in a demanding field.

11.4 Marketing and Creative Fields

Interviews in marketing and creative fields often assess your creativity, strategic thinking, and ability to deliver results. Be prepared to showcase your portfolio and discuss specific campaigns or projects.

Key Focus Areas:
   1. Portfolio Review: Be ready to walk through your best work and explain your creative process.

2. Strategic Thinking: Demonstrate how you approach marketing challenges and develop effective strategies.

3. Data Analysis: Show how you use data to inform creative decisions and measure campaign success.

4. Trend Awareness: Display knowledge of current marketing trends and emerging platforms.

5. Collaboration: Highlight experiences working with diverse teams (e.g., designers, copywriters, data analysts).

Sample Questions:
   - "Tell me about a marketing campaign you're particularly proud of. What was your role, and what were the results?"
   - "How do you stay creative when working within brand guidelines or tight deadlines?"
   - "Describe how you would approach marketing a new product to a millennial audience."

Tips:
   - Have a well-organized, easily accessible portfolio (digital or physical).
   - Be prepared to give an elevator pitch for a product or service on the spot.
   - Familiarize yourself with the company's brand and recent marketing campaigns.
   - Be ready to discuss both traditional and digital marketing strategies.

11.5 Education

Education interviews often focus on teaching philosophy, classroom management skills, and ability to engage diverse learners. Be prepared to discuss specific teaching methodologies and your approach to student development.

Key Focus Areas:
1. Teaching Philosophy: Articulate your approach to education and how it aligns with the institution's values.

2. Lesson Planning: Be ready to discuss or demonstrate how you plan and execute effective lessons.

3. Classroom Management: Share strategies for creating a positive learning environment and handling behavioral issues.

4. Technology Integration: Discuss how you incorporate technology into your teaching.

5. Assessment Methods: Explain your approach to evaluating student progress and providing feedback.

Sample Questions:
- "How do you differentiate instruction to meet the needs of diverse learners?"
- "Describe a challenging student behavior you've encountered and how you addressed it."
- "How do you incorporate current events or real-world applications into your lessons?"

Tips:
- Be prepared to give a sample lesson or "micro-teach" session.
- Research the school or institution's educational philosophy and curriculum.
- Highlight any experience with special education or English language learners.
- Be ready to discuss how you engage with parents and the broader school community.

11.6 Non-Profit Sector

Non-profit interviews often assess your passion for the cause, ability to work with limited resources, and skills in relationship building and fundraising.

Key Focus Areas:
  1. Mission Alignment: Demonstrate genuine interest in and commitment to the organization's mission.

  2. Resource Management: Show how you maximize impact with limited resources.

  3. Fundraising: Highlight any experience in grant writing, donor relations, or fundraising campaigns.

  4. Stakeholder Management: Discuss your approach to working with diverse stakeholders, including volunteers, donors, and community partners.

  5. Impact Measurement: Show understanding of how to measure and communicate program effectiveness.

Sample Questions:
  - "What draws you to our organization's mission?"
  - "Describe a successful fundraising campaign you've been involved in. What made it effective?"
  - "How do you approach building partnerships with other organizations or community leaders?"

Tips:
  - Research the organization's programs, recent initiatives, and major donors.
  - Be prepared to discuss current trends and challenges in the non-profit sector.

INDUSTRY-SPECIFIC INTERVIEW GUIDES

   - Highlight any volunteer experience or personal connections to the cause.
   - Demonstrate understanding of the unique challenges and rewards of working in the non-profit sector.

General Tips for All Industries:

1. Research the Company:
   - Understand the company's mission, recent projects, and industry position.
   - Be prepared to discuss why you're interested in this specific organization.

2. Know the Role:
   - Thoroughly review the job description and be ready to relate your experiences to the key responsibilities.

3. Prepare Industry-Specific Examples:
   - Have concrete examples ready that demonstrate your skills and experiences relevant to the industry.

4. Stay Current:
   - Be aware of current trends, challenges, and innovations in your industry.
   - Be prepared to discuss how these might impact the role or organization.

5. Understand the Culture:
   - Research the company culture and be ready to discuss how you would fit in.

6. Prepare Thoughtful Questions:
   - Have industry-specific questions ready that demonstrate your knowledge and interest.

7. Highlight Transferable Skills:
   - If transitioning from another industry, focus on how your skills and experiences translate to this new sector.

8. Show Passion:
   - Demonstrate genuine enthusiasm for the industry and the specific role.

9. Continuous Learning:
   - Highlight your commitment to ongoing professional development in your field.

10. Tailor Your Communication Style:
    - Adjust your language and examples to fit the industry. For example, use more technical language in IT interviews, or focus on patient outcomes in healthcare.

Remember, while these guides provide a starting point for industry-specific preparation, each company and role is unique. Always tailor your preparation to the specific position and organization you're interviewing with. Pay attention to the job description, company website, and any other information you can gather about the role and the organization's current priorities.

Additionally, be prepared to discuss how recent events or trends have impacted your industry. For example, in healthcare, you might discuss the impact of telemedicine; in education, the shift to online learning; or in tech, the growing importance of cybersecurity.

By combining these industry-specific insights with the general interview preparation techniques discussed in earlier chapters, you'll be well-equipped to excel in interviews across a variety of sectors. Remember to stay authentic, showcase your unique experiences and perspectives, and demonstrate how your skills and passion align with the needs of the role and the organization.

The Future of Interviews: Staying Ahead of the Curve

As technology continues to evolve and reshape the business world, the landscape of job interviews is also undergoing significant changes. Understanding these emerging trends and preparing for them can give you a competitive edge in your job search. This chapter explores the future of interviews, focusing on AI-driven interviews, virtual reality interviews, and other emerging trends.

12.1 AI-Driven Interviews: What to Expect

Artificial Intelligence (AI) is increasingly being used in the hiring process, including in interviews. AI-driven interviews can take various forms, from chatbots conducting initial screenings to AI analysis of video interviews.

Key Aspects of AI-Driven Interviews:

1. Video Analysis:
   - AI can analyze facial expressions, tone of voice, and word choice during video interviews.
   - It may assess factors like confidence, stress levels, and engagement.

2. Natural Language Processing:
   - AI can evaluate your responses for relevance, coherence, and depth of

knowledge.
   - It may analyze your language patterns and vocabulary usage.

3. Personality Assessments:
   - AI might infer personality traits based on your responses and behavior during the interview.

4. Skill Evaluations:
   - Some AI systems can administer and evaluate skill-based tests or coding challenges.

5. Bias Reduction:
   - AI is sometimes used with the goal of reducing human bias in the hiring process, although it's important to note that AI systems can also inherit biases if not carefully designed.

How to Prepare for AI-Driven Interviews:

1. Practice with AI Tools:
   - Familiarize yourself with AI interview platforms by using practice tools available online.

2. Focus on Clear Communication:
   - Speak clearly and concisely, as AI may have difficulty interpreting complex or ambiguous language.

3. Be Mindful of Non-Verbal Cues:
   - Practice maintaining good eye contact with the camera and positive body language.

4. Prepare Structured Responses:
   - Use frameworks like STAR (Situation, Task, Action, Result) to structure your answers, as AI often looks for clear, logical responses.

5. Highlight Keywords:
   - Incorporate relevant keywords from the job description into your responses, as AI may be programmed to look for these.

6. Be Authentic:
   - While it's important to be prepared, avoid overly rehearsed responses that might come across as unnatural to AI analysis.

7. Test Your Technology:
   - Ensure your camera, microphone, and internet connection are working well to avoid technical issues that could affect AI's analysis.

Ethical Considerations:

It's worth noting that the use of AI in hiring decisions raises ethical questions and concerns about privacy and fairness. Be aware of your rights and don't hesitate to ask the company about how your data will be used and stored.

12.2 Virtual Reality Interviews: The Next Frontier

Virtual Reality (VR) interviews are an emerging trend that could become more common in the future, especially for roles that require specific spatial or interactive skills.

Key Aspects of VR Interviews:

1. Immersive Environments:
   - Interviews might take place in virtual offices or customized environments relevant to the job.

2. Skill Demonstrations:
   - VR can allow for hands-on demonstrations of skills in a simulated environment.

3. Scenario-Based Assessments:
   - Candidates might be placed in virtual scenarios to assess their decision-making and problem-solving skills.

4. Remote Collaboration:
   - VR can simulate collaborative tasks, allowing interviewers to assess teamwork skills.

5. Cultural Fit Evaluation:
   - Virtual office tours or team interactions could be used to gauge cultural fit.

How to Prepare for VR Interviews:

1. Familiarize Yourself with VR:
   - If possible, practice using VR technology before the interview.

2. Focus on Spatial Awareness:
   - Be prepared to navigate and interact in a 3D environment.

3. Practice Verbal Communication:
   - In VR, clear verbal communication becomes even more important as some non-verbal cues may be lost.

4. Prepare for Unexpected Scenarios:
   - Be ready to think on your feet and adapt to unique virtual situations.

5. Maintain Professionalism:
   - Remember that even in a virtual environment, professional behavior is crucial.

6. Address Motion Sickness:
   - If you're prone to motion sickness in VR, consider mentioning this to the

interviewer beforehand.

7. Dress Appropriately:
   - Even though you'll be in VR, you might be visible to interviewers, so dress professionally.

Potential Challenges:
   VR interviews are still in early stages and may present technical challenges or accessibility issues. Be prepared to discuss alternatives if needed.

12.3 Emerging Interview Trends and How to Prepare

Beyond AI and VR, several other trends are shaping the future of interviews. Here are some to be aware of:

1. Asynchronous Video Interviews:
   - Candidates record responses to preset questions on their own time.
   - Preparation: Practice recording yourself and reviewing your performance. Focus on concise, engaging responses.

2. Gamified Assessments:
   - Game-like tests to evaluate skills, cognitive abilities, and personality traits.
   - Preparation: Stay calm and approach these as you would any other assessment. Practice logical thinking and quick decision-making skills.

3. Social Media Screening:
   - Companies increasingly review candidates' online presence.
   - Preparation: Audit your social media profiles. Ensure they present a professional image aligned with your career goals.

4. Collaborative Assignments:
   - Group interviews or projects to assess teamwork and leadership skills.
   - Preparation: Practice active listening, clear communication, and con-

structive collaboration. Be prepared to take initiative without dominating.

5. Continuous Evaluation:
   - Some companies are moving towards ongoing assessment rather than one-off interviews.
   - Preparation: Maintain consistent professionalism and enthusiasm throughout all interactions with the company.

6. Personality and Emotional Intelligence Assessments:
   - Increased focus on soft skills and cultural fit.
   - Preparation: Reflect on your interpersonal skills and emotional responses. Be prepared to discuss how you handle various social situations.

7. Diversity and Inclusion Focus:
   - Companies are placing greater emphasis on building diverse teams.
   - Preparation: Be ready to discuss your experiences working in diverse environments and your approach to inclusion.

8. Skills-Based Hiring:
   - Less emphasis on formal qualifications, more on demonstrable skills.
   - Preparation: Be ready to showcase your skills through portfolios, projects, or practical demonstrations.

9. Automated Scheduling and Follow-ups:
   - AI-driven systems managing interview logistics.
   - Preparation: Be responsive and flexible. Double-check all automated communications for accuracy.

10. Holistic Candidate Evaluation:
    - Companies considering a wider range of factors beyond just interview performance.
    - Preparation: Ensure consistency across all touchpoints with the company, from application to follow-up.

THE FUTURE OF INTERVIEWS: STAYING AHEAD OF THE CURVE

General Preparation Strategies for Future Interviews:

1. Stay Technologically Adept:
   - Keep up with new technologies and platforms. Be comfortable with video conferencing, collaborative tools, and potentially VR/AR applications.

2. Develop Your Digital Presence:
   - Cultivate a professional online presence. This might include a personal website, active LinkedIn profile, or professional portfolio.

3. Focus on Adaptability:
   - Highlight your ability to learn quickly and adapt to new situations. This skill will be increasingly valuable as interview formats evolve.

4. Enhance Your Emotional Intelligence:
   - Work on understanding and managing your emotions, as well as recognizing emotions in others. This will be crucial in both AI-analyzed and human interviews.

5. Practice Data-Driven Self-Presentation:
   - Be prepared to back up your claims with concrete data and measurable achievements.

6. Develop Strong Narrative Skills:
   - Practice telling compelling stories about your experiences and skills. Narrative ability will remain important even as technology advances.

7. Cultivate a Growth Mindset:
   - Show your commitment to continuous learning and improvement. This attitude will be valuable in any future interview scenario.

8. Ethics and AI Awareness:
   - Develop an understanding of AI ethics and be prepared to discuss the

implications of AI in your field.

9. Cross-Cultural Competence:
   - As remote work enables more global hiring, develop your ability to communicate effectively across cultures.

10. Wellness and Stress Management:
    - As interviews become more complex and potentially more stressful, focus on developing strong stress management skills.

Ethical Considerations in Future Interviews:

As interview technologies advance, it's important to be aware of potential ethical issues:

1. Data Privacy:
   - Understand how your data is being collected, used, and stored during the interview process.

2. Algorithmic Bias:
   - Be aware that AI systems can inherit biases. If you feel you've been unfairly assessed, don't hesitate to seek clarification.

3. Accessibility:
   - If new interview technologies present accessibility challenges for you, communicate this to the employer. Companies should provide alternatives.

4. Informed Consent:
   - Ensure you understand and agree to how new technologies will be used in your interview process.

5. Right to Human Evaluation:
   - Some jurisdictions are considering laws that give candidates the right to

human evaluation in hiring decisions. Stay informed about your rights.

Conclusion:

The future of interviews is likely to be a blend of human interaction and technological assistance. While the fundamentals of presenting yourself professionally and demonstrating your skills will remain important, the methods of evaluation are evolving rapidly.

Staying ahead of these trends involves not just familiarity with new technologies, but also developing the soft skills that are becoming increasingly important in the modern workplace. Adaptability, emotional intelligence, and strong communication skills will serve you well regardless of the interview format.

Remember, despite technological advances, the core purpose of an interview remains the same: to find the best match between a candidate and a role. By understanding and preparing for these emerging trends, you can present your best self in any interview format, positioning yourself for success in the evolving job market.

As you encounter new interview technologies or methods, approach them with an open mind and a willingness to learn. Your ability to adapt and thrive in changing circumstances is itself a valuable skill that employers will appreciate. Stay informed, stay prepared, and you'll be ready to excel in the interviews of the future.

Interview Success Stories: Learning from the Best

Success in job interviews often comes from a combination of preparation, adaptability, and the ability to learn from both successes and failures. This chapter explores real-life interview success stories and the valuable lessons we can extract from top performers across various industries.

13.1 Case Studies of Remarkable Interview Turnarounds

Case Study 1: The Power of Persistence and Self-Improvement

Sarah, a software engineer, had been rejected after three rounds of interviews with a leading tech company. Instead of getting discouraged, she asked for feedback, which revealed that her technical skills were strong, but she struggled to communicate complex ideas clearly.

Action Taken:
   - Sarah joined a local Toastmasters club to improve her public speaking skills.
   - She started a tech blog to practice explaining technical concepts in simple terms.
   - She contributed to open-source projects to gain more collaborative coding experience.

Result:

Six months later, Sarah reapplied to the same company. This time, she excelled in all rounds, impressing interviewers with her clear communication and collaborative approach. She was offered the position with a higher salary than initially discussed.

Key Lesson: Treat rejections as learning opportunities. Specific, actionable feedback can be the key to dramatic improvement.

Case Study 2: Turning a Perceived Weakness into a Strength

Mark was a career changer, moving from teaching to marketing. In initial interviews, he struggled to convince employers that his lack of traditional marketing experience wasn't a liability.

Action Taken:
   - Mark created a presentation showcasing how his teaching skills translated to marketing (e.g., understanding audience needs, crafting compelling narratives).
   - He completed several marketing certifications to show his commitment to the field.
   - He volunteered to manage social media for a local non-profit, gaining practical experience.

Result:

In his next interview, Mark proactively addressed his unconventional background. He presented his unique perspective as an asset, showing how his teaching experience could bring fresh ideas to marketing strategies. The company was impressed by his initiative and innovative thinking, and he was offered the job.

Key Lesson: Don't shy away from what makes you different. Find ways to present your unique experiences as valuable assets.

Case Study 3: Overcoming Interview Anxiety

Jennifer was a highly qualified accountant who consistently underperformed in interviews due to severe anxiety.

Action Taken:
- Jennifer sought help from a career counselor who specialized in interview anxiety.
- She practiced mindfulness and breathing techniques to manage stress.
- She conducted numerous mock interviews with friends and mentors, gradually increasing the pressure to simulate real conditions.

Result:
In her next interview, Jennifer was able to manage her anxiety effectively. She came across as confident and composed, allowing her qualifications and personality to shine. She received job offers from two of the three companies she interviewed with.

Key Lesson: Interview skills can be developed and improved. Addressing underlying issues like anxiety can dramatically change interview outcomes.

Case Study 4: Mastering the Art of Storytelling

Carlos was a project manager with a solid track record, but he struggled to make an impact in interviews, often giving vague or overly technical answers.

Action Taken:
- Carlos worked with a career coach to develop a repertoire of compelling stories that showcased his achievements.
- He practiced the STAR method (Situation, Task, Action, Result) to structure his responses.
- He created a "brag book" with visual aids and data to support his stories.

Result:

In his next series of interviews, Carlos was able to engage interviewers with vivid, relevant examples of his work. His stories clearly demonstrated his skills and problem-solving abilities. He received multiple job offers and was able to negotiate a higher salary based on the value he convincingly presented.

Key Lesson: Concrete, well-structured stories are powerful tools in interviews. They make your achievements memorable and relatable.

13.2 Lessons from Top Performers Across Industries

While every industry has its specificities, top performers in interviews often share common traits and strategies. Here are key lessons from successful interviewees across various sectors:

1. Thorough Preparation

Lesson: Success in interviews starts long before you enter the room.

Examples:
   - A top-performing sales executive creates a mock product pitch for every interview, tailored to the company's specific challenges.
   - A software engineer review common algorithmic problems and practices explaining their thought process out loud.
   - A marketing professional researches the company's recent campaigns and comes prepared with ideas for improvement.

Action Points:
   - Research the company extensively, including recent news, challenges, and competitors.
   - Prepare concrete examples of your achievements, tailored to the job requirements.

- Practice common interview questions, focusing on clear, concise responses.

2. Emotional Intelligence

Lesson: The ability to read and connect with interviewers can set you apart.

Examples:
- A successful HR manager pays close attention to the interviewer's body language and adjusts her communication style accordingly.
- A project manager demonstrates active listening skills, building rapport through thoughtful follow-up questions.
- A customer service representative showcases empathy in her responses, a key trait for her role.

Action Points:
- Practice active listening during interviews.
- Pay attention to non-verbal cues and adjust your approach if necessary.
- Show genuine interest in the interviewer and the company.

3. Adaptability and Quick Thinking

Lesson: The ability to handle unexpected questions or situations impresses interviewers.

Examples:
- A finance professional, when faced with a surprise case study, calmly talks through his problem-solving process.
- An IT consultant, when asked about a technology she's unfamiliar with, honestly admits her lack of knowledge but outlines how she would quickly learn it.
- A teacher, in a panel interview with contradicting viewpoints, diplomatically addresses all perspectives in her response.

Action Points:
- Practice thinking on your feet with unexpected interview questions.
- If you don't know something, be honest and explain how you would find the answer.
- Stay calm under pressure; your reaction to stress is often more important than having all the answers.

4. Demonstrating Cultural Fit

Lesson: Top performers show alignment with the company's values and culture.

Examples:
- A startup candidate demonstrates his entrepreneurial spirit by discussing side projects and innovations.
- A corporate lawyer highlights her experience in collaborative environments when interviewing with a firm known for teamwork.
- A graphic designer for a socially conscious brand showcases personal projects aligned with social causes.

Action Points:
- Research the company culture thoroughly.
- Prepare examples that demonstrate your alignment with the company's values.
- Ask questions that show you're considering how you'll fit into the team.

5. Showing Growth Mindset and Continuous Learning

Lesson: Employers value candidates who are committed to ongoing development.

Examples:
- A data scientist discusses how she keeps up with rapidly evolving

technologies in her field.

- A healthcare administrator shares how he implemented lessons from a recent leadership seminar in his current role.

- A digital marketer showcases certifications she's earned in emerging platforms.

Action Points:
- Highlight recent learning experiences or new skills you've acquired.
- Discuss how you stay updated in your field.
- Show enthusiasm for growth opportunities within the potential role.

6. Turning Weaknesses into Opportunities

Lesson: How you discuss your weaknesses can demonstrate self-awareness and problem-solving skills.

Examples:
- A project manager discusses how she overcame her tendency to micromanage by implementing new delegation strategies.
- A sales representative shares how he improved his initially poor time management skills with specific productivity techniques.
- A designer explains how feedback on her weaker coding skills motivated her to take online courses in front-end development.

Action Points:
- Be honest about areas for improvement, but focus on steps you're taking to address them.
- Frame weaknesses as challenges you're actively working to overcome.
- Provide specific examples of how you've grown from past mistakes or shortcomings.

7. Asking Thoughtful Questions

Lesson: The questions you ask can be as important as the answers you give.

Examples:
   - A business analyst asks about the biggest data-related challenges the team is currently facing.
   - An operations manager inquires about opportunities for process improvement within the organization.
   - A UX designer asks about the company's approach to user research and testing.

Action Points:
   - Prepare a list of thoughtful questions that demonstrate your knowledge and interest.
   - Ask questions that show you're thinking about how you can contribute to the company's success.
   - Use questions as an opportunity to highlight your strengths indirectly.

8. Following Up Effectively

Lesson: The interview process doesn't end when you leave the room.

Examples:
   - A marketing coordinator sends a personalized thank-you email referencing specific points from the interview and adding additional thoughts.
   - A software developer follows up with links to projects they discussed during the interview.
   - A sales manager sends a brief, tailored proposal based on challenges mentioned during the interview.

Action Points:
   - Send a thank-you note within 24 hours of the interview.
   - Reference specific points from the interview to show attentiveness and interest.

- If appropriate, provide additional information or work samples that support your candidacy.

9. Resilience and Positivity

Lesson: Maintaining a positive attitude, even in the face of challenging interviews, is crucial.

Examples:
   - A teacher candidate, after a tough question, takes a moment to compose herself and then provides a thoughtful answer.
   - A finance professional, when faced with a critical comment about his resume, responds with grace and provides context that turns the perceived negative into a positive.
   - An engineering manager, after an initial rejection, maintains contact with the company and is considered for (and wins) a better-fitting role months later.

Action Points:
   - Practice maintaining composure in stressful interview simulations.
   - View every interview as a learning experience, regardless of the outcome.
   - Stay positive and professional in all interactions, even if you feel the interview isn't going well.

Conclusion:

These success stories and lessons from top performers illustrate that interview success is not about luck or innate talent. It's about thorough preparation, continuous improvement, and the ability to present your authentic self in the best possible light.

Key takeaways include:
   - Preparation is crucial, but so is the ability to adapt in the moment.

- Every interview, regardless of the outcome, is an opportunity to learn and improve.

- Soft skills like emotional intelligence and communication are often as important as technical qualifications.

- Authenticity, combined with strategic presentation of your strengths, is key to making a lasting impression.

- The interview process extends beyond the interview itself – preparation before and follow-up after are critical components of success.

By studying these examples and implementing these lessons, you can significantly improve your interview performance. Remember, becoming a top performer in interviews is a skill that can be developed with practice, reflection, and a commitment to continuous improvement.

The 30-Day Interview Preparation Plan

Preparing for a job interview is not just about the days leading up to the big day. A comprehensive, structured approach over a longer period can significantly boost your confidence and performance. This 30-day plan is designed to systematically improve your interview skills, covering all aspects of interview preparation.

14.1 Week-by-Week Guide to Interview Readiness

Week 1: Self-Assessment and Research

Day 1-2: Self-Assessment
  - Review your career goals and how this job aligns with them.
  - List your key strengths, skills, and achievements.
  - Identify areas for improvement or skill gaps.

Day 3-5: Company and Industry Research
  - Thoroughly research the company: history, culture, recent news, products/services.
  - Analyze the industry: trends, challenges, major players.
  - Study the job description in detail, noting key requirements and responsibilities.

Day 6-7: Network and Gather Intel
  - Reach out to contacts who work in the company or industry.

- Use LinkedIn to research your potential interviewers and team members.
- Prepare questions about the company and role based on your research.

Week 2: Crafting Your Narrative

Day 8-9: Develop Your Personal Brand
- Craft your personal pitch (elevator pitch).
- Align your personal brand with the company's values and culture.

Day 10-11: Prepare Your Stories
- Develop 5-7 stories using the STAR method (Situation, Task, Action, Result) that showcase your key achievements and skills.
- Ensure these stories are relevant to the job requirements.

Day 12-13: Refine Your Resume and Online Presence
- Update your resume to align with the job description.
- Review and update your LinkedIn profile and other professional online presence.

Day 14: Practice Verbal Communication
- Record yourself answering common interview questions.
- Focus on clear articulation, appropriate pace, and engaging tone.

Week 3: Interview Skills and Techniques

Day 15-16: Master Common Interview Questions
- Practice answering common interview questions.
- Prepare for behavioral and situational questions.

Day 17-18: Industry-Specific Preparation
- Research and practice industry-specific technical questions.
- Prepare examples of your expertise relevant to the role.

Day 19-20: Salary Negotiation Preparation
   - Research salary ranges for the position and industry.
   - Practice discussing salary expectations and benefits.

Day 21: Non-Verbal Communication
   - Practice maintaining good eye contact, posture, and hand gestures.
   - Work on projecting confidence through body language.

Week 4: Mock Interviews and Final Preparation

Day 22-23: Conduct Mock Interviews
   - Arrange for mock interviews with friends, family, or a career coach.
   - Record these sessions for self-review.

Day 24-25: Review and Refine
   - Review your mock interview performances.
   - Refine your answers and body language based on feedback.

Day 26-27: Prepare Interview Materials
   - Organize copies of your resume, references, and work samples.
   - Prepare your interview attire and ensure everything is ready.

Day 28: Final Company Research
   - Check for any recent news or updates about the company.
   - Refine your questions for the interviewer based on your research.

Day 29: Mental Preparation
   - Practice relaxation techniques.
   - Visualize a successful interview.

Day 30: Final Review
   - Review key points about the company and position.
   - Go over your prepared stories and answers.

- Get a good night's sleep.

14.2 Daily Exercises to Build Interview Muscle

Incorporating daily exercises into your 30-day plan can help reinforce your preparation and build your "interview muscle." Here are exercises you can rotate through each day:

1. Elevator Pitch Practice (5 minutes)
   - Refine and practice your 30-second personal pitch.
   - Try different versions for various contexts (networking, interview opening, etc.).

2. STAR Story Development (10 minutes)
   - Choose a different accomplishment each day.
   - Structure it using the STAR method.
   - Practice telling it concisely and engagingly.

3. Industry News Review (15 minutes)
   - Read industry-related news articles or blogs.
   - Reflect on how this information might be relevant in an interview.

4. Question Preparation (10 minutes)
   - Prepare and refine questions to ask your interviewer.
   - Ensure they demonstrate your research and genuine interest in the role.

5. Mock Interview Question (5 minutes)
   - Answer one mock interview question out loud.
   - Record your answer and listen back for areas of improvement.

6. Body Language Check (5 minutes)
   - Practice your posture, handshake, and eye contact in a mirror.
   - Work on aligning your facial expressions with your words.

7. Technical Skill Review (15 minutes)
   - Review a technical skill relevant to the job.
   - Prepare an example of how you've used this skill in a professional context.

8. Company Research Deep Dive (10 minutes)
   - Choose one aspect of the company (a product, service, or recent initiative) to research in-depth.
   - Prepare talking points about how this aligns with your interests or experience.

9. Networking Outreach (10 minutes)
   - Reach out to a professional contact or alumnus working in your target industry.
   - Prepare questions about their role or company.

10. Salary Research (10 minutes)
    - Research salary data for your target role and industry.
    - Practice articulating your salary expectations based on this research.

11. Stress Management Exercise (5 minutes)
    - Practice a quick stress-relief technique (deep breathing, progressive muscle relaxation, etc.).
    - This will be valuable for managing pre-interview nerves.

12. Weakness Reframing (10 minutes)
    - Identify a professional weakness and practice discussing it constructively.
    - Focus on steps you're taking to improve in this area.

13. Achievement Quantification (10 minutes)
    - Choose a professional achievement and practice quantifying its impact.
    - Use specific numbers and data to make your accomplishment more concrete.

14. Interview Etiquette Review (5 minutes)
   - Review best practices for interview etiquette (arrival time, greeting, thank-you notes, etc.).
   - Prepare your plan for following these best practices.

15. Personal Anecdote Preparation (10 minutes)
   - Prepare a brief, engaging personal anecdote that showcases a key personality trait relevant to the job.
   - Practice telling it in under two minutes.

16. Company Culture Alignment (10 minutes)
   - Identify aspects of your work style or values that align with the company's culture.
   - Prepare examples that demonstrate this alignment.

17. Problem-Solving Scenario (15 minutes)
   - Create a hypothetical work problem relevant to the role.
   - Practice walking through how you would approach solving it.

18. Active Listening Practice (10 minutes)
   - Listen to a short podcast or video related to your industry.
   - Practice summarizing the key points, as you might need to do in an interview.

19. Failure Analysis (10 minutes)
   - Reflect on a professional failure or setback.
   - Practice discussing what you learned from it and how you've grown.

20. Leadership Example (10 minutes)
   - Prepare an example of when you demonstrated leadership, even if not in a formal leadership role.
   - Focus on the impact of your actions.

21. Conflict Resolution Scenario (15 minutes)
    - Develop a scenario involving workplace conflict.
    - Practice explaining how you would handle it professionally.

22. Technology Check (10 minutes)
    - If preparing for a video interview, test your technology setup.
    - Practice looking at the camera and managing your background.

23. Interview Closing Statement (5 minutes)
    - Prepare and practice a strong closing statement for your interview.
    - Include a summary of your interest and fit for the role.

24. Thank-You Note Draft (10 minutes)
    - Draft a template for your post-interview thank-you note.
    - Customize it with space to add specific details from the interview.

25. Creativity Exercise (10 minutes)
    - Choose a common object and brainstorm uncommon uses for it.
    - This helps develop quick, creative thinking useful in interviews.

26. Professional Goal Articulation (10 minutes)
    - Practice articulating your short-term and long-term professional goals.
    - Align these with the potential for growth within the company.

27. Unexpected Question Preparation (5 minutes)
    - Have someone ask you an unexpected, off-the-wall question.
    - Practice remaining composed and giving a thoughtful answer.

28. Positive Visualization (5 minutes)
    - Visualize yourself succeeding in the interview.
    - Imagine feeling confident, articulate, and engaged.

29. Rapid-Fire Skills List (5 minutes)

- Set a timer and quickly list as many of your relevant skills as possible.
- This helps internalize your strengths for quick recall during the interview.

30. Passion Project Discussion (10 minutes)
    - Prepare to discuss a personal project or interest.
    - Focus on how it demonstrates qualities relevant to the job (e.g., initiative, creativity).

By following this 30-day plan and incorporating these daily exercises, you'll systematically improve all aspects of your interview performance. This comprehensive approach addresses not just the content of your answers, but also your mental preparation, body language, and overall presentation.

Remember, consistency is key. Dedicate time each day to these exercises, and you'll find your confidence and competence growing steadily. By the time your interview arrives, you'll be well-prepared to present your best self and make a strong, positive impression.

Conclusion: From Interview Success to Career Triumph

As we conclude this comprehensive guide to mastering interviews, it's important to recognize that the skills you've developed are not just for landing a job – they're foundational to long-term career success. This final chapter will explore how to leverage your newly honed interview skills for ongoing professional growth and how to maintain and improve these skills throughout your career.

15.1 Leveraging Your New Skills for Long-Term Success

The skills you've developed in preparing for interviews are highly transferable to many aspects of your professional life. Here's how you can leverage these skills for long-term career success:

1. Effective Communication
   - In Interviews: You've learned to articulate your experiences and skills clearly and concisely.
   - For Career Success: Apply this skill in daily interactions, presentations, and when pitching ideas to colleagues or superiors.

Action Steps:
   - Volunteer to present at team meetings or industry conferences.
   - Practice summarizing complex ideas in simple terms.

CONCLUSION: FROM INTERVIEW SUCCESS TO CAREER TRIUMPH

- Seek opportunities to communicate with different departments to broaden your impact.

2. Self-Awareness and Personal Branding
 - In Interviews: You've developed a strong sense of your strengths, weaknesses, and unique value proposition.
 - For Career Success: Use this self-awareness to guide your career decisions and personal development.

Action Steps:
 - Regularly reassess your skills and how they align with your career goals.
 - Develop a personal development plan based on your identified areas for improvement.
 - Cultivate your personal brand within your organization and industry.

3. Research and Analysis Skills
 - In Interviews: You've honed your ability to research companies and industries thoroughly.
 - For Career Success: Apply these skills to stay ahead of industry trends and make informed decisions.

Action Steps:
 - Set up news alerts for your industry and key competitors.
 - Regularly analyze market trends and their potential impact on your role and company.
 - Use your research skills to identify new opportunities for innovation within your organization.

4. Storytelling and Example-Driven Communication
 - In Interviews: You've practiced crafting compelling stories to illustrate your achievements.
 - For Career Success: Use storytelling to make your ideas more engaging and memorable in workplace communications.

Action Steps:
- Incorporate relevant anecdotes in your reports or presentations.
- Use the STAR method to structure your contributions in meetings.
- Mentor junior colleagues by sharing your experiences through well-crafted stories.

5. Adaptability and Quick Thinking
- In Interviews: You've prepared for unexpected questions and scenarios.
- For Career Success: Apply this adaptability to navigate change and solve problems efficiently in your role.

Action Steps:
- Volunteer for cross-functional projects to expose yourself to new challenges.
- Practice brainstorming solutions to hypothetical work problems.
- Develop a methodology for approaching unfamiliar tasks or situations.

6. Networking and Relationship Building
- In Interviews: You've learned to build rapport quickly with interviewers.
- For Career Success: Extend this skill to build a strong professional network within and outside your organization.

Action Steps:
- Attend industry events and conferences regularly.
- Set up informational interviews with colleagues from different departments.
- Cultivate relationships with mentors and potential mentees.

7. Goal Setting and Achievement Orientation
- In Interviews: You've articulated your career goals and aligned them with potential roles.
- For Career Success: Apply this goal-oriented mindset to your current role and long-term career planning.

Action Steps:
- Set SMART (Specific, Measurable, Achievable, Relevant, Time-bound) goals for your current role.
- Develop a five-year career plan and review it annually.
- Seek regular feedback on your progress towards your goals.

8. Confidence and Self-Promotion
- In Interviews: You've learned to speak confidently about your achievements.
- For Career Success: Use this skill to advocate for yourself in the workplace and take on new challenges.

Action Steps:
- Keep a record of your accomplishments and review it regularly.
- Practice discussing your achievements with colleagues and superiors.
- Seek out opportunities to take on more responsibility or lead projects.

9. Active Listening and Emotional Intelligence
- In Interviews: You've honed your ability to read between the lines and pick up on non-verbal cues.
- For Career Success: Apply these skills to improve your relationships with colleagues, superiors, and clients.

Action Steps:
- Practice reflective listening in meetings and one-on-one interactions.
- Pay attention to team dynamics and work on improving interpersonal relationships.
- Seek feedback on your emotional intelligence and work on areas for improvement.

10. Stress Management and Resilience
- In Interviews: You've developed techniques to manage interview anxiety.
- For Career Success: Use these skills to maintain high performance under

pressure in your daily work.

Action Steps:
   - Incorporate stress-management techniques into your daily routine.
   - Develop a personal resilience plan for dealing with setbacks or high-pressure situations.
   - Practice reframing challenges as opportunities for growth.

15.2 Continuous Improvement: Keeping Your Interview Skills Sharp

Even after landing your desired job, it's crucial to maintain and improve your interview skills. These skills are valuable for internal promotions, networking, and potential future job searches. Here's how to keep your interview skills sharp:

1. Regular Self-Assessment
   - Schedule quarterly self-reviews to assess your skills and achievements.
   - Update your resume and LinkedIn profile with new accomplishments and skills.

2. Mock Interviews
   - Participate in mock interviews at least once a year, even when not actively job searching.
   - Ask a trusted colleague or mentor to conduct these interviews and provide feedback.

3. Stay Current with Industry Trends
   - Set aside time each week to read industry publications and news.
   - Attend webinars or conferences to stay updated on the latest developments in your field.

4. Networking Practice
   - Attend networking events regularly to practice your elevator pitch and

small talk skills.
   - Seek out opportunities to speak at industry events or contribute to professional publications.

5. Continuous Learning
   - Take online courses or pursue certifications relevant to your field.
   - Learn new skills that complement your current role and prepare you for future opportunities.

6. Mentor Others
   - Offer to mentor junior colleagues or participate in mentorship programs.
   - Teaching others reinforces your own knowledge and communication skills.

7. Seek Feedback
   - Regularly ask for feedback from colleagues, superiors, and subordinates.
   - Use this feedback to identify areas for improvement and track your progress.

8. Practice Storytelling
   - Continuously update your repertoire of professional stories and achievements.
   - Practice incorporating these stories into your daily professional communications.

9. Stay Tech-Savvy
   - Keep up with new technologies relevant to your industry and job search processes.
   - Familiarize yourself with the latest video interviewing platforms and digital presentation tools.

10. Volunteer for New Challenges
    - Take on projects outside your comfort zone to broaden your experience

and skills.
 - Volunteer for cross-functional teams or committees within your organization.

11. Role-Play Difficult Conversations
 - Practice handling difficult workplace scenarios through role-play exercises.
 - This could include conflict resolution, negotiation, or giving constructive feedback.

12. Maintain a Growth Mindset
 - Approach each professional interaction as a learning opportunity.
 - Reflect on your experiences and extract lessons for future improvement.

13. Update Your Interview Questions
 - Regularly revise the questions you ask in professional settings.
 - Stay informed about current events and industry changes to ask relevant, insightful questions.

14. Practice Salary Negotiations
 - Even if you're not actively job searching, practice articulating your value and negotiating compensation.
 - This skill is valuable for annual reviews and internal promotions.

15. Engage in Professional Writing
 - Write articles for professional publications or maintain a blog on industry topics.
 - This hones your ability to articulate complex ideas clearly and builds your professional brand.

Implementing a Continuous Improvement Plan:

1. Set Quarterly Goals

CONCLUSION: FROM INTERVIEW SUCCESS TO CAREER TRIUMPH

- Identify specific interview and professional skills you want to improve each quarter.
- Set measurable objectives for each goal.

2. Create a Learning Schedule
   - Allocate time each week for skill development and industry research.
   - Balance this with your work responsibilities to ensure consistency.

3. Seek Opportunities to Practice
   - Volunteer to introduce speakers at company events.
   - Offer to represent your team in cross-departmental meetings.

4. Reflect and Adjust
   - After each significant professional interaction (presentation, meeting, networking event), reflect on your performance.
   - Identify what went well and areas for improvement.

5. Build a Support Network
   - Form a peer group focused on professional development.
   - Share experiences, practice skills together, and provide mutual feedback.

6. Track Your Progress
   - Maintain a journal of your professional development activities and insights.
   - Regularly review this to see how far you've come and identify patterns in your growth.

7. Stay Accountable
   - Share your professional development goals with a mentor or trusted colleague.
   - Schedule regular check-ins to discuss your progress and challenges.

Conclusion:

The journey from interview success to career triumph is an ongoing process of growth, learning, and adaptation. By leveraging the skills you've developed through interview preparation – from effective communication and self-awareness to adaptability and continuous learning – you can position yourself for long-term career success.

Remember that these skills are not static; they require regular practice and refinement. By committing to continuous improvement and staying attuned to industry trends and personal growth opportunities, you'll not only maintain your interview readiness but also enhance your overall professional capabilities.

Your career is a marathon, not a sprint. Each interaction, whether it's a formal interview, a team meeting, or a casual networking event, is an opportunity to apply and refine these skills. Approach your career with the same level of preparation, enthusiasm, and strategic thinking that you've applied to your interview preparation.

By doing so, you'll not only be ready for your next big opportunity but you'll also maximize your potential in your current role. You'll become a valued team member, an insightful leader, and a professional who's always prepared to take the next step in their career journey.

Embrace the mindset of continuous growth, stay curious, and never stop honing your skills. Your commitment to ongoing improvement will not only prepare you for future interviews but will also pave the way for a fulfilling and successful career. Remember, every day is an opportunity to interview for your next big role – even if that role is an enhanced version of the position you currently hold.

www.ingramcontent.com/pod-product-compliance
Lightning Source LLC
Chambersburg PA
CBHW050303230526
45471CB00005B/2003